Walks Through History

in the Heart of England

A collection of fascinating circular
trails around some of the best
heritage sites in the region

by

Roger Seedhouse

ENGLISH
HERITAGE
Membership
offer
See page 149

Meridian Books

Published 2001 by Meridian Books

© Roger Seedhouse 2001

ISBN 1-869922-41-7

A catalogue record for this book is available from the British Library.

The right of Roger Seedhouse to be identified as the author of this work has been asserted by him in accordance with the Copyright, Designs and Patents Act 1988.

Maps based upon the Ordnance Survey maps with the permission of the Controller of Her Majesty's Stationery Office. Crown Copyright.

Meridian Books
40 Hadzor Road, Oldbury, West Midlands B68 9LA

Printed in Great Britain by MFP Design & Print, Manchester

Contents

Introduction

AS we moved towards the third millennium, hurtling ever faster into cyberspace, I began to feel there was a real danger that we would all become too pre-occupied with the world of virtual reality to remember our past. Such a trend could ultimately be detrimental to mankind itself and perhaps this book will help in a very small way to redress the balance.

The Heart of England is rich in history, both ancient and more modern. From iron-age forts to medieval castles to second world war camps. Many of them remain relatively undiscovered yet will offer the visitor an intriguing glimpse into a bygone age. I often think of the classic film starring Rod Taylor based upon the H.G.Wells novel *The Time Machine* and wish I could turn the clock back to witness the events which shaped our history or that took place at the site in question. The tumult of battle, life in a stone age village, grand living on a Victorian estate – all these things and more could be experienced if only I had the right bits and pieces to assemble! Except that, in the film, time advanced and I don't think the future was portrayed as something to look forward to.

I hope you enjoy the walks. Please read the information section at the start of each walk as it will help you to decide which one is the most suitable at the time and assist planning.

Roger Seedhouse

The Walks

THE majority of the twenty-four walks are based upon English Heritage sites, although I have included a few others because of their particular interest. The whole of the five counties of the West Midlands are covered together with two sites in Gloucestershire and one site in Leicestershire and, with motorway connections now, they should all be readily accessible wherever you live.

Distances vary from 3 miles up to 13½ miles (although this can be divided up to create two separate walks). All of them contain places of interest which you may wish to explore so please allow adequate time to complete the walks, particularly the longer ones where the best part of a day will be required. The type of terrain also differs considerably and I have tried to give some guidance as to what to expect in the introductions.

Grid references (GR) for the starting points are given in the introduction to each walk. If you are unfamiliar with the use of these you will find details on Ordnance Survey Landranger and other maps.

Reference points on the sketch maps are shown in the text thus: ❶

Points to consider

1. Wear sensible gear. A good pair of boots is essential; so are waterproofs and warm clothing in less clement weather or when undertaking wild hill walks.

2. If you can, take a map of the area. Landranger (1:50,000 or 1¼ inches to the mile) is the most commonly used but Explorer or the older Pathfinder (both 1:25,000 or 2½ inches to the mile) with much more detail are better. I am not suggesting this because you are likely to get lost but merely as a prudent precaution just in case you do stray off the route or if, perhaps because of deteriorating weather, you want to cut short the walk. A compass is also a valuable item for the same reasons.

3. Some paths, particularly those less well used, can get overgrown in summer. A walking stick can make life a lot easier ·in such situations and, sometimes, a pair of secateurs. A small first aid kit should also be carried in the event of a close encounter with a bramble or other mishap.

4. The countryside is constantly changing. Seasonal changes can make things which appear obvious or easy to recognise in summer less so in winter and vice-versa. Be wary also of physical changes. The position or type of gate/fence/stile may be altered, field boundaries are changed or even removed altogether, tracks can be diverted (officially or otherwise), etc.

5. A Right of Way is precisely what it says – you have the right to walk along it at all times unimpeded. Fortunately, most County Councils pursue a continuing programme of clearing and waymarking paths, but this is a huge task and many remain obscure. Likewise, most landowners adopt an enlightened attitude towards walkers but occasionally obstructions will be encountered, paths will have been obliterated or diverted or not

reinstated after planting has taken place. Try not to be daunted by such things and remember that you have a legal right to pass. Needless to say, common sense should come to the fore in such situations; for example, it may be necessary to take a path around the edge of a cropped field rather than across it or follow an unofficial diversion rather than stick to the line on the map. Any serious obstructions should, however, be reported to the local Council's Rights of Way department.

6. Some animals can create consternation for the walker. Farm dogs are frequently encountered but mostly make a lot of noise rather than cause any physical injury. Again, a walking stick is useful just to be on the safe side. A field of frisky young bullocks is best avoided. Even though they are merely curious or think you have come to feed them, I prefer to skirt around them where possible. Sheep are no problem!

7. Not many pub landlords like muddy boots trampling over their floors. Try to be considerate and, if you cannot clean them off, take them off and leave outside or in a lobby.

8. Last, but not least, REMEMBER THE COUNTRY CODE!

Public transport services to some areas are very limited or even non-existent. Some appropriate telephone numbers are:

British Rail: 0345 484950
Centro (West Midlands trains and buses): 200 2700
Travel Line: (Buses and Coaches) 0870 608 2608

GOOD WALKING!

About the Author

Roger Seedhouse is a Chartered Surveyor and a partner in a firm of property consultants in the West Midlands. He has lived on the border of Shropshire and Staffordshire all his life and has an extensive knowledge of the Midlands counties. When not ministering to the requirements of his two daughters his spare time is divided between Rotary Club activities and walking.

He is the author of two other books of walks, *Walks to Wet your Whistle* and *More Walks to Wet your Whistle*.

English Heritage Sites

Admission to all properties visited on these walks is free to English Heritage members. For non-members admission prices vary from site to site. There are three levels: Adult/Concession/Children under 16. Current prices and opening times are given in the information boxes included in the relevant chapters.

Concessions are available for senior citizens, unemployed people on production of UB40 and students on production of student union card.

Children under five are admitted free.

In the information boxes

EH indicates an English Heritage site,

NT indicates a National Trust site

Useful websites:

www.english-heritage.org.uk   www.nationaltrust.org.uk

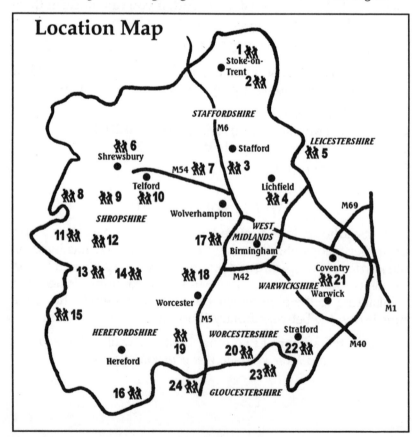

Location Map

1

The Mines and Caves of the Manifold Valley

Maps: Outdoor Leisure (yellow cover) 24.
Start: The small car park by the bridge at Wettonmill (not the car park to the mill itself). To get there turn off the A523 about four miles to the south-east of Leek along the northbound section of the B5053. After a further three miles or so take a right through the village of Butterton towards Wetton. The lane descends steeply to a junction in front of the River Manifold with Wettonmill opposite. Turn left here to gain the car park on your right. GR 096561.
Distance: 6½ miles (although it may feel longer!).
Terrain: A fascinating wander along part of the Manifold valley with a return via the abandoned copper mines of Ecton and mysterious prehistoric caves cut out of the limestone cliffs above the valley, all set in the spectacular scenery of Staffordshire Moorlands. The first part of the route is flat but there are some fairly stiff climbs later where firm foothold is required. Do not attempt the walk if totally inexperienced or in any way unfit.
Refreshments: Café at Wettonmill. There is a pub (Ye Olde Royal Oak) in the village of Wetton.

FROM the car park walk along the lane northwards following the course of the River Manifold and the route of the former Leek and Manifold Light Railway. Beforehand you can visit Wettonmill across the bridge – the redundant corn mill here has not been restored so there is not a lot to see, but note the cave on the outcrop above. This contained animal remains from the late glacial period, about 80,000 years BC, and the Stone Age. You will see this again later from an entirely different perspective.

After about a mile and a quarter of walking through this pleasant landscape you go through Swainsley Tunnel, the only tunnel on the L&MVLR, which provided a passenger and freight service from Waterhouses to the south up to Hulme End some 8½ miles to the north between 1904 and 1934. It was never profitable. Incidentally, the river is crossed twenty-eight times along its route and the tunnel was constructed to prevent the railway spoiling the view from Swainsley Hall! Care is required while passing through the tunnel as it is single track only with no footpath, but it is lit.

When you emerge from the tunnel the lane loops right but you should continue straight ahead across a footbridge over Warslow Brook and through a gate onto a narrow tarmac footpath to continue with the River Manifold on your right. This

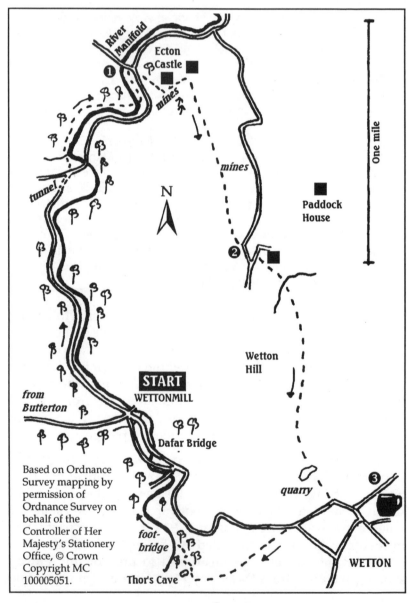

is a pretty tree lined track (still the route of the L&MVLR) which rises above the river then descends to meet it again. After a while you will see ahead the spoil heaps of the old Ecton Copper Mines, but more of that a little later. You cross two footbridges after which the track opens out to reach a junction with a lane. **①**

Here turn right but after only a few yards turn right again at another junction and then, after a further distance of only some 15 yards, bear off left following the public footpath sign to Top of Ecton and Wetton. This is a broad track leading uphill and reaches a most unusual stone built property in gothic style, which reminded me of something out of a Hammer House of Horrors movie. It is, in fact, a folly and if you look carefully you will see that it bears the date 1931. It was called 'Ecton Castle' and is now used as an educational establishment and contains a museum relating to the mining industry in the area which you will see evidence of very shortly. There is a choice of ways here – take the option straight ahead across the front of the property, under an arch then turn left before reaching a gate and cross a stile into a steep field.

Once in the field keep close to the left boundary and do not be tempted to bear half right on a path which leads around the rear of a plantation of fir trees. The climb is steep and at times could be slippery, so some caution is required. At the top is a large fenced off mineshaft and a deserted cottage as well as a spectacular view backwards over the Manifold Valley. You walk ahead for a few yards to meet a crossing fence line where views open out to the north and east with numerous villages dotting the Moorlands landscape. Here turn 90 degrees right to follow a more gentle upward course with the fence on your left. Along the way you will pass many fenced off shafts on a ridge which offers further excellent views on both sides although it will feel exposed in inclement weather.

At some 1400 feet, the Ecton Copper Mine was once the deepest in Britain and one of the largest in Europe, producing almost a million tons of ore during its era. The area was first mined by the Romans but the most productive period was during the 1700s and 1800s. It closed in 1890 following a collapse in the price of copper and lead. PLEASE NOTE that disused mines are very dangerous and on no account should any of the shafts or openings be entered. Children and pets are particularly at risk.

You go through a squeeze stile in a crossing boundary and continue along a grassy track before passing more shafts on the left with Wetton Hill in view ahead. Go through another squeezer at the end of a dry stone wall and continue the line forward over open moorland heading towards more mine workings. When you arrive there you will find a stile and a choice of routes. Continue ahead to the right of the quite extensive old workings with the extremely neat farm complex of Paddock House below on your left. The way now descends to the left of a dry stone wall to reach a gate onto a lane where you turn left. ❷

You shortly reach a junction with another lane and turn left again. After a distance of about 80 yards the lane bottoms out and here turn sharp right at a waymark post in front of a cottage into a field. Follow the left boundary on a narrow path which can be slippery in wet weather and at the end, under some trees, is another waymark post. The ground around here can get, and probably is, boggy at any time so be prepared! Go left here to cross a track (ignoring the waymark on the right) and negotiate a stile into the adjacent field.

Cross the field directly aiming towards the bottom right corner in a dip where there is a stile to cross into the National Trust area of Wetton Hills. Now stay ahead passing to the left of a small group of trees to enter on a rising path towards two ridges ahead. There is a dry stone wall in view and you join this to continue onwards and upwards between the two ridges. As the ground starts to level out a little you pass through a wooden squeeze stile and then depart from the dry stone wall by veering half left over an enclosed field.

In the opposite boundary you can see another squeezer and you go through this to climb a rocky path before proceeding on a somewhat indistinct way through a field with patchwork fields enclosed by dry stone walls on your right. Go through a squeeze stile at the end of the field and stay ahead across a quarry site then through yet another squeezer to reach a gate leading onto a tarmac track to the left of a small covered reservoir. This takes you down to the pretty Moorlands village of Wetton where you can, if you wish, take refreshment at the Ye Olde Royal Oak pub (turn left). ❸

Otherwise, turn right and at the end of the village is a signposted junction where you keep ahead on the lane towards

Wettonmill and Butterton. After 30 yards bear left onto a narrow track waymarked 'Thor's Cave' with a sign advising that this is a concessionary path and is used at your own risk. Follow the track as it winds between dry stone walls and crosses a step stile alongside a wooden gate to continue downhill. After another 50 yards or so you cross another step stile over a dry stone wall on your right, just beyond a gate, then turn left with a waymark to gently descend in a field.

Go through a gap in a crossing boundary to continue in the next field following a clear path which rises to a stile alongside an ash tree in the far boundary. Once over take the right hand descending track which drops down to the right of a cliff face. Be very careful here as the track is narrow and slippery in places. At the base of the cliff the main, and newly stepped path to Thor's Cave joins from the right but you continue upwards for a few yards to arrive at the impressive entrance to the cave.

After completing your visit to the cave enter on the stepped downward course and stay on it to reach a junction where you

Thor's Cave

turn left to continue the descent. At the bottom you cross a footbridge then bear right onto a tarmac 'lane' back in the river valley and the route of the L&MVLR. This last three quarters of a mile of the route is likely to be extremely busy at certain times and you may need to take evasive action against cyclists. However, don't let that spoil your enjoyment.

You now have the River Manifold for company again although, according to a visitor leaflet it is supposed to invisible along this section, apparently disappearing on a subterranean course just to the north of Dafar Bridge (which you will reach shortly) and re-appearing at Ilam Hall to the south. However, on two occasions I have visited the area to research this walk the river was definitely flowing overground, if at a reduced rate. It had been raining heavily on both occasions and it was in wintertime, so perhaps there is overflow and underflow in very wet conditions.

You pass Ossoms Crags on your left before crossing a footbridge and turning left to continue alongside the river. Next cross Dafar Bridge and stay on the lane back to Wettonmill. You are obliged to cross a stream which runs across the road before getting back but, if you don't fancy that you can divert around it via a footbridge over to your left.

Thor's Cave

THE entrance to Thor's Cave is 30ft high and the width 23ft and is set in a huge limestone cliff which was once the home of prehistoric man. When inside (where great care is required) you may be able to imagine the scene of 10,000 years ago depicted by many illustrations. Numerous artefacts have been found here from the Neolithic, Celtic, Roman and Anglo- Saxon periods and these are now on display at museums in Buxton and Hanley.

A large pillar of limestone, shaped like a tree, stands inside the cave and light enters via an opening known as the west window. Thor's Fissure Cave, located to the south of the window was excavated in the 1920s and yielded many bones from bears, wolves and polecats as well as human skulls and copious pottery. The two riverside caves below are said to have been used as stables by supporters of Bonnie Prince Charlie in 1745 on their retreat from Derby. One further thing – from outside you can see in the distance the cave above Wettonmill mentioned at the beginning of the walk.

Staffordshire

2

Froghall

Maps: Landranger 119, 128; Pathfinder 810; Explorer 258, 259.
Start: From the car park at Froghall Wharf, which is just off the
A52, 10 miles to the east of Stoke-on-Trent, on the lane leading
towards the village of Foxt. GR 026476.
Distance: 6½ or 8½ miles.
Terrain: A fascinating trail through the archaeology of this once
booming canal-side industrial centre, starting with a stretch of the
Caldon Canal which displays many relics of the former mining
activity, followed by a walk along the Staffordshire Moorlands
Way with some superb views over the Churnet Valley. Return via
the old Plateway used to transport limestone from the Caldon
Low quarries down to Froghall Wharf. One stiffish climb on the
first part.
Refreshments: There is a small shop at Froghall Wharf selling
drinks/icecream. Otherwise, a short diversion en route into the
village of Foxt will reveal the Fox & Goose public house, a
pleasantly situated establishment serving meals and bar snacks.

Froghall Wharf

FROGHALL WHARF is a history lesson in itself. For nearly a
century it was a hive of industrial activity, handling what was
described as an inexhaustible supply of limestone from the
quarries 3½ miles away at Caldon Low. To enable the wagons
to be brought down to canal level a series of tracks was built using
inclined planes to traverse the steepest sections as well as a cable
railway. You will see the remains of some of these along the route of
the walk

It all started in 1778 with completion of the Caldon Canal
between Stoke-on Trent and Froghall and the Tramway to the
quarries which was used by horse drawn wagons. This consisted of
iron strips fixed to wood on a foundation of stone but, by 1783, it was
considered badly placed and superseded by a Plateway which was
basically a double line of plates laid on stone blocks. Limestone was
smelted in the huge kilns still visible at the Wharf and loaded onto
barges for use in building and in blast furnaces.

At their height in the mid to late nineteenth century, the quarries
were producing up to 1,000 tons of limestone per day but in 1905 a
new standard gauge railway link was constructed direct to the

7

quarries and thereafter the wharf declined in importance. The last of the tracks linking the wharf with the quarries was closed in 1920. There are a number of information boards at the Wharf which tell the story in more detail.

FROM the main car park, cross the road through the smaller car park opposite and enter on the Caldon Canal towpath. You emerge to cross Ipstones Road directly and continue along the towpath running adjacent to the Thomas Bolton factory. Once past this the scene becomes more attractive and you might spare a thought for the efforts of Staffordshire County Council and Stoke City Council who, in partnership with British Waterways and the Caldon Canal Society, have restored this disused section of canal for recreational use. The Canal was originally opened in 1778, the year the first rail line to the limestone quarries was completed, as no doubt you will have already have gathered from the information board at the wharf.

After about another half mile you will pass a stile on the left with the River Churnet visible below and shortly afterwards arrive at Cherryeye Bridge, so named because the eyes of local miners were reddened by iron ore dust from ironstone which was extracted nearby. See the grooves cut into the timber posts on the underside of the bridge by centuries of ropes pulling barges.

The railway line to your left is presently unused although a restoration project is underway to create an extension to the

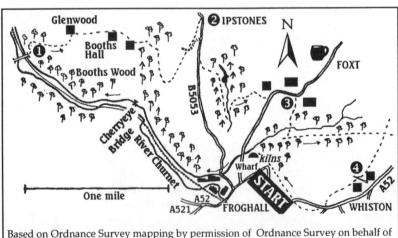

Based on Ordnance Survey mapping by permission of Ordnance Survey on behalf of the Controller of Her Majesty's Stationery Office, © Crown Copyright MC 100005051.

North Staffordshire Railway which runs from Cheddleton near Leek down to Consall Forge just to the north of here. The next landmark is a steel girder bridge which you are obliged to cross before continuing on the opposite side of the canal. After 50 yards look for a jutting boulder with its petrified water – don't put your hand in it lest you turn to stone! Providing you have heeded my warning you will shortly thereafter reach a ruined flint mill on the opposite side which appears to be in a state of slow restoration. Stay on the towpath under another steel girder bridge (No. 51) and just beyond a mile post and before the next bridge, leave the towpath by climbing up a stepped embankment to the right to reach a broad stone track. ❶

Booth's Wood

Cross the track directly following the signs for Booth's Wood Walk on the 'red' waymarked route. You climb up another flight of steps into deciduous woodland and onto part of the Staffordshire Moorlands Route. After a fairly stiff climb you reach level ground and walk along a ridge for a short while through pleasant woodland. As the area to your left opens out into a field, look carefully for a stile which takes you into the said field and follow the left boundary of it (the waymark at the stile is misleading as it suggests following the right boundary). There are one or two home made signs to show you the way and please ignore the stile in the corner after 50 yards.

At the top of the field go through a gate and bear left onto a broad stony track going around to the rear of Glenwood Farm. Pass between stone farm buildings and turn right directly opposite the farmhouse along another stony track. Again there are signs to assist. You don't follow this track for long – after a few yards stay with the fence line to the left field boundary to reach an electricity pole and waymark about 100 yards away then cut half right to the next pole in the centre of the field and on to the next, adjacent to which is a stile. This is somewhat superfluous as there is nothing either side of it! Now follow a farm track to the right of a field boundary heading towards Booths Hall.

Before getting to the farm a waymark directs you left over a stile. There is a choice of routes here and you need to keep tight on the right boundary of a field, with the village of Ipstones in view to your left, passing to the left of a new bungalow and, at the top of the field, cross another stile to proceed on a metalled farm track to the right of a chicken coop. Go though an open gateway to the left of corrugated barns then over a fence stile at the rear of them onto another stony track leading to yet another farm. Do not go up to the farm but bear almost immediately left in the adjacent field to skirt around the left of the buildings. After about 70 yards cross a stile on the right then turn left on a path leading away from the farm towards a belt of trees.

As the ground dips towards the trees do not be tempted to go through a gate on your left but continue down the dip to cross a stile in the tree line. This takes you onto a path leading steeply down into an attractive wooded valley. There are steps for most of the way and, when you reach the bottom, cross a footbridge to climb a short flight of steps and over another stile. You now have to scramble up an embankment (which can get slippery) before

10

turning right onto a narrow path between trees. This soon broadens out as you climb to exit from the wood via another stile. From here follow the waymark half left across a field to join and continue with a dry stone wall.

You shortly go over a stile and, after another 100 yards, look for a waymarked fence stile on your left crossing the stone wall into the adjacent field. The stile is fairly rough! Cross this adjacent field directly to the left of two gate openings on the opposite side. Go through this gate then cross the next field to a squeeze stile 120 yards ahead in a jutting corner. You go through another squeezer and ahead to the right of a dry stone wall with views over Staffordshire Moorlands to your right.

At the end of the wall go forward on the gravelly farm track on a gradual descent closing with the road to your right. As the track loops right towards the road DO NOT GO WITH IT ALONG THE OBVIOUS ROUTE (although it would save some time and distance if you did!); instead veer off left across pasture field to a stile in the left hedge about 80 yards away. Again its a squeeze stile and take care not to prickle something on the holly hedge! Once through continue the line forward diagonally across the next field to a gateway in a dry stone wall alongside which is yet another squeezer. Go through onto the road and turn right. ❷

You immediately come to a blind bend and it is probably best to cross the road here and walk along the grass verge for a while before re-crossing. There is no footpath so care is required. After about a third of a mile bear left over a waymarked stile by a gate onto a stony track to the right of some trees. Follow the track down to cross a stile by a gate to enter mixed woodland and, after a while, you will see a pool down to the left. The pool is in fact a quarry pool and there are a number of disused shafts in the locality. You descend gradually keeping ahead at a junction and on reaching level ground, just before a waymark post, bear off left over a brook. This path is *not* waymarked. Follow it as it loops left and rises on a fairly stiff climb.

Continue ahead where the tree line ends on the left along a narrower path which can get a bit overgrown. You go through another squeeze stile almost at the top and stay ahead with a hedge on your right. After about another 120 yards you arrive at a crossing hedge and a waymarked gate – here turn right onto a grassy path between hedgerows and keep going through or round a number of gates before emerging onto a lane to the right of some cottages.

You can cut short the walk from here by turning right along the lane for about half a mile back to the car park but that would be a pity as there is plenty more to come. If intending to go the distance bear left past what was The Woodcutter public house towards Foxt. The lane climbs then levels out to pass an attractive row of Victorian villas where there are good views back over Froghall. About 100 yards past the Post Office on the right go right down a waymarked tarmac track. Alternatively, if you could manage some refreshment, stay on the lane for a third of a mile into Foxt where you will find the Fox and Goose, then reverse steps to the tarmac track referred to. **❸**

The track descends to the right of a row of cottages after which the surface turns to stone/grass. You go round a gate and quickly through a second gate but, take a little care over direction now. The waymark at this last gate is misleading and tends to suggest that you should follow the most obvious route alongside a hedge across the top of a valley; this is not correct – instead continue the descent keeping to your left by a mixed tree boundary. This is quite a steep path and you very gradually move away from the left boundary and skirt to the right of a tongue of mixed trees (the path can get overgrown in summer) after which point the way loops right to reach a stile and bridge over a brook. Cross and continue until reaching a fork in front of a new house and bear left up some steps to reach a crossroads with a broader stony track.

Turn left and proceed on what will become a fairly long climb. *This is the line of the former Cable Railway, the last wagonway built between the quarries and Froghall Wharf and used between 1849 and 1920 when the limestone contract with ICI was terminated. Each train had nine wagons carrying six tons of limestone and were linked by cables wound round drums at the top of the incline. The laden wagons descending pulled the empty ones up the slope.* Keep ahead where the sandstone cliff ends on your right after which the track crosses the first of the wagon tracks consisting of wood laid on a foundation of stone. These wagons were drawn by horses. Go under a sandstone bridge and through a squeeze stile then another after a further 80 yards. Eventually you reach more level ground at the top of the incline where there is a crossing right of way.

There is a large and curious sandstone boulder in the field to the left but we need to go right into a field along a path to the right of a dry stone wall. At the end of this long field you cross a stile and veer half right in the next field to go through a gap in another dry stone wall on the opposite side in line with farm buildings to the rear. Keep the same line towards the farm and in the angle of the stone wall in front of the farmhouse is a stone squeeze stile which you go through to reach a junction with a metalled lane running through the farm. **4**

Turn right onto the lane and, at the end of the buildings, bear left through another stone squeezer into a field following a downward course to the right of a dry stone wall. At the end of the field go through a further squeezer and turn right to go through another after 40 yards to proceed to the left of a dry stone wall. Just before the end of this field go through a squeeze stile on your right and continue in the same direction but with dry stone wall on your left. Go through yet another squeezer after 80 yards and stay ahead in the next field curving down to the lower left corner. Pass through a gate on the left here and follow a grassy farm track for about 120 yards before passing through yet another squeeze stile in a fence 10 feet to the right of a gate to emerge onto the A52.

Turn right and after 100 yards bear left down a grassy track almost opposite a defunct garage. This is the line of the Plateway and you follow it almost back to the car park. *The Plateway was the second of the three lines constructed to link the Wharf to Caldon Low Quarries and consisted of a double line of plates laid on stone blocks. Horses pulled the wagons on level sections but drums and cables were used on slopes. Operations ceased in 1849.* You go through an archway under a house, which was probably built for use by cable operators, then down one of the inclines into a wood. Cross a lane at the bottom by the main road and go over a stile and then another to stay on the descending course through trees. *This is the Great Froghall Plane and drops nearly 250 feet in 300 yards and carried the wagons downhill on the 1802 plateway, dividing at the base with one branch going to the lime-kilns and the other continuing down to the canalside.* Go through a gap between a cottage and stone building (possibly an original shelter for machinery used on the incline) then turn left and immediately right opposite the cottage following a waymark by the lime-kilns back to the car park.

3

Tɧe Cannock Cɧase War Trail

Maps: Explorer 6 – Cannock Chase and Chasewater.
Start: The car park at Coppice Hill nearby the village of Brockton, which itself is about four miles south-east of Stafford just off the A34. Turn right at the village green in Brockton then immediately left uphill and, after climbing for around half a mile and passing the entrance to a quarry, bear left along another lane signed Coppice Hill and continue to the parking area right at the end. GR 979192.
Distance: 7½ miles.
Terrain: A glimpse of more recent history with a trail through the legacy of the Great War, mainly on well used paths over part of one of the premier areas of natural beauty in the Midlands. Some excellent views with a little climbing in parts, although nothing too taxing. The Chase tends to be heavily used at times, particularly on fine days at weekends so, if possible, go midweek. It also makes a superb winter walk but take care not to run out of daylight.
Refreshments: There is a café at Springslade Lodge – see route plan.

Cannock Chase

CANNOCK CHASE covers an area of 28 square miles wedged between Stafford and Cannock. In 1958 it was designated an Area of Outstanding Natural Beauty and it is certainly well qualified for this status by virtue of a wonderful variety of woodland, moorland and escarpments with sweeping views across the Midland plain. The name Cannock is thought to derive from the Celtic 'Cnoc', meaning a hill or high ground and the Chase was an ancient hunting ground used by the Anglo-Saxon rulers of Mercia. It is recorded in the Domesday Book as belonging to the King but it ceased to be a royal forest at the end of the thirteenth century when it passed to the Bishop of Lichfield. At one time it covered a huge area, including Lichfield, Walsall and part of Wolverhampton. Some of the oak trees surviving from the ancient forest can still be seen as indeed can deer and a rich variety of flora and fauna.

To apply a description of 'natural beauty' is slightly misleading in that much of the Chase is now covered by Forestry Commission plantations. It must also be borne in mind that, at the start of the twentieth century, it was very different to the way it is now – extremely bleak with barren landscape and none of the now familiar afforestation. During the first World War it accommodated two huge Army Training camps for troops destined for the trenches. Up to half a million men passed through the camps and as many as 1500 huts blanketed the top of the Chase.This walk takes you on a journey around some of what remains of these camps and incorporates the Commonwealth and German War Cemeteries. It is a pity that the remains have been neglected and some are now barely visible because of vegetation – perhaps one day some public spirited Authority or individual will instigate a clearance and restoration project so that this important feature of local history and the part it played in the great conflict is not entirely forgotten.

THE car park itself is located on a former training parade ground. From there walk back down the access roadway for about 100 yards, just past a direction indicator post on the left, and turn left through a smaller car parking area and out onto a grassy path. After a further 100 yards or so turn right at a junction. Look carefully to your right after another 100 yards to find *Freda's Grave* – the mascot of the New Zealand Rifles 1918. Freda was a Dalmatian and her collar and lead are kept in a military museum in New Zealand.

Continue on the path towards the road again and, on your left just before reaching it, the undulating ground marks the lines of the *Women's Auxiliary Corps* hut lines. Bear left on the road and after some 350 yards you will pass another parking area. Just beyond that note over to your left embankments marking the line of *Tackeroo*, the now dismantled camp railway which linked the various buildings and service facilities. You will see much more evidence of this on other stages of the walk. Just after the parking area on the left is a long flat grassy area, underneath which is the concrete base of the *Ordnance Store*. Again the *Tackeroo* cutting is clearly visible to the rear and, in fact, there was also a station here where ammunition and uniforms were unloaded into storage.

Turn left across this flat area and out the back of it to arrive immediately at the *Glacial Boulder* which stands on the base of what was a huge *Reservoir Tower* which supplied water for the trains. The ice age boulder originates from Scotland and was placed here in the 1950s. To the rear is a trig. point and close to the rear of that runs a broad waymarked track where you will see

15

there is a junction between the Staffordshire Way and the Heart of England Way. Turn right here, effectively joining the latter (not the grassy path to the sharp right). From here, on a clear day, there are views left over a huge swathe of countryside stretching up to North Staffordshire and the Moorlands. Keep right at a fork after 150 yards and at the waymarked crossroads in another 250 yards bear right again to follow a gradually descending track towards Chase Road Corner car park. Before getting there, veer off right on a narrower path down to the remains of the *Coal Store*. Daily rations of fuel for heating and cooking were issued from here with the railway high up to the rear to help unloading. Proceed now over to the car park and turn right to go through it for the short distance to the roadway. To your left on the raised area of ground once stood the *Veterinary Hospital* and the *Officers' hut lines* but, regrettably, most of what remains is obscured by undergrowth. **❶**

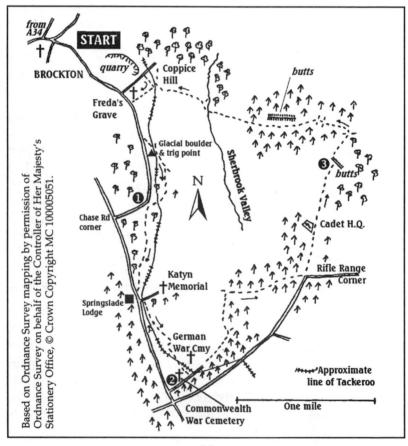

The Glacial Boulder

You don't actually need to join the roadway before veering off left down a waymarked track and following it for, perhaps a little over half a mile to a junction with a road with Springslade Lodge Café opposite. On your left here (opposite the café) is a narrow surfaced lane signed *Katyn Memorial* which you will reach after only 100 yards or so. This memorial is dedicated to the 14,000 members of the Polish armed forces and others who where executed in Katyn Forest in 1940.

From the Katyn Memorial re-trace your steps back towards the road but, 20 yards before getting there, turn left along a track which initially runs parallel with it. Ignore a crossing path as the track climbs gradually then opens out with a clear view of the Telecom Tower ahead. You need to zig-zag right then left before going through a car park and out onto another track on the far side. On your left you will shortly see the embankments marking another section of *Tackeroo* before reaching a junction with another lane. Turn right for 250 yards to visit the *Commonwealth War Cemetery*, where many German, New Zealand and British servicemen who died in the camp hospitals were buried, then re-trace your steps along the metalled lane past your exit onto it and after a short distance you will arrive at the *German War Cemetery and Visitor Centre*. It is here where, in 1967, the remains of all German servicemen who died in Britain in both wars were brought for re-burial – a total of 2143 from the first war and 2797 from the second. A silent and thought provoking place. **❷**

On leaving the German Cemetery turn left to continue on the metalled lane. This soon deteriorates to stone and, upon reaching a fork, keep left along the lower path then stay with the path as it bears round to the right by a waymark. After a further 250 yards you will reach a crossroads and turn right along a broader track and the Heart of England Way. Follow this for about half a mile keeping right at a fork to reach a junction with a road at Rifle Range Corner. Just before getting to the road turn 90 degrees left along a very broad, straight track.

Keep ahead at a Forestry Commission sign to the right of the Cadet H.Q. and ahead again as the track loops left to the rear of it. Ignore all side tracks and continue for some half a mile to arrive at the *second world war rifle butts*. At least I believe they are second war although if I am wrong no doubt someone will correct me! Apparently they were in use until quite recently. We were fortunate to be alone on our visit here and found it to be enormously atmospheric. I could almost see the ghosts of troops lined up on the bank in front and hear the deafening noise of rifle fire. **❸**

Cross in front of the butts and turn right to take the track going away at the rear. After about a quarter of a mile you reach a broad forestry track and cross it directly into a pine wood. This leads down to a junction where you take the least obvious route straight across on a narrower path which shortly brings you to a junction with another broad track. Cross that directly on a rising stony path though a fir plantation and, after a steady climb, go ahead at a crossroads to reach yet another crossroads after a further 250 yards. If you turn right here a short distance will bring you to the second of the *Rifle Ranges*. It is much larger than the first and extends fully the 250 yards parallel to the path between the two crossroads. This one originates from the Great War and, if you take a closer look it will be apparent that this end is rather better preserved than the other. Again an atmospheric and desolate place – I wonder how many soldiers of the first War put through their training here actually came back from the trenches?

Re-trace your steps to the last crossroads and turn right to continue on the track you were previously following. Where the trees end continue ahead on the track opposite which leads down into Sherbrook Valley. Ignore all side paths until you get down into the valley where you cross the brook via a footbridge and turn right at a junction with a broader path. This is a pretty area popular for family outings but do not carried away and miss your next direction after only a matter of 60 yards or so. Here there is a waymarked crossroads of paths where you continue more or less ahead on the Staffordshire Way along a rising track.

After a fairly stiff climb you reach a junction and turn right on a path which will lead back to Coppice Hill car park. You can cut right to reach it without having to meet the driveway.

Staffordshire

4

Roman Wall

Maps: Landranger 139; Pathfinder 892; Explorer.
Start: The English Heritage car park just off the A5 about a mile to the east of its junction with the A461 Walsall-Lichfield road at Muckley Corner. Wall Roman Site is signed at the turn off point. GR 097065.
Distance: 5½ miles.
Terrain: Easy going along mainly (there is one exception!) well used paths with some good views across the wedge of countryside towards Sutton Coldfield.
Refreshments: There is a public house in Wall and several in Shenstone.

EH   **Wall**   **NT**

A S is well known the A5, or Watling Street, marks the route of the great Roman military road from Kent to North Wales and Wall (Letocetum) became an important staging post along that route. The settlement's essential purpose was to provide accommodation and a change of horses for Roman officials but it grew into a small trading post with an extended range of facilities, including the public bath house the remains of which can be seen along with those of the Inn and Mansio (hostel). There is an on site museum showing many of the excavated artefacts.

If you have time and are not already familiar with the area I would suggest a visit to the City of Lichfield and its magnificent Cathedral, which is only about two and a half miles to the north. I would like to have been able to devise a walk route linking the present day city of Lichfield with the former Roman city of Wall but, unfortunately, this was not practical.

The site is owned by the National Trust but managed by English Heritage
Open: 1 April to 30 Sept, 10am to 6pm; 1 to 31 October, 10 am to 5 pm.
Admission: £2.30/ £1.70/ £1.20. Includes taped guide .
Tel: 01543 480768.

START the walk by going along the lane to the side of the car park and turn almost immediately right along a waymarked track called 'Roman Walk' which leads you out along a field edge to the rear of the site. It continues to the left of the wall to St. John's Church to exit at a junction with a lane and here turn right. A key is available if you wish to visit the church, otherwise continue past it for about 30 yards then bear left down Market Lane. After passing through an attractive residential area you will reach a junction and turn right until arriving at another junction with Claypit Lane after a further 150 yards. Cross directly onto a broad waymarked bridleway.

There are some good views to the right along this track and you may be able to see the Sutton Coldfield Transmitter and the village of Shenstone, where you will in due course arrive, with its prominent church towers. Pity about the row of pylons! You enter a grassy track between hedgerows and can now see ahead the Lichfield Transmitter. Go under the railway bridge (beware, this could be muddy) and shortly afterwards exit via a gate onto an-

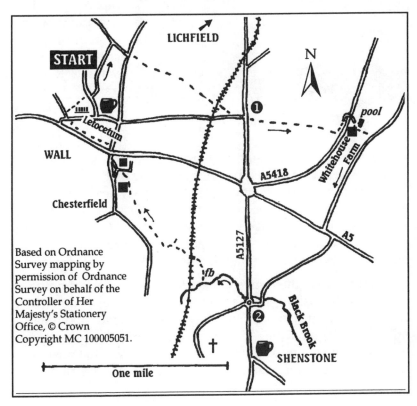

The path to Wall Church

other lane. Turn left for a little over 100 yards and, on reaching a junction with the A5127, cross directly through gates onto another broad farm track. ❶

You will shortly go under the pylons referred to after which you may see the three spires of Lichfield Cathedral protruding above the landscape to your left. At a point where the path turns left across the field, continue the line straight ahead. Stay on the path as it narrows along the field edge and, when you reach the corner, you are obliged to wiggle right between fence posts then left before continuing on the same line as before but now to the right of a field boundary heading towards the A5148. At the bottom bear left to re-cross the boundary and walk along the field edge bordering the main road. This leads you onto a track and over a bridge across the road then, on the other side, it continues in the direction of Whitehouse Farm.

You arrive at the farm and bear left along a track running to the right of a fishing pool which shortly exits at another lane where a right turn is required. Stay on the lane for about half a mile until it joins the A5 – turn left along the grass verge bordering the main road but, you will be relieved to know, only for 100 yards before carefully crossing to take the right turn

Wall Roman Town

towards Shenstone. Just before reaching the built-up area you will pass Shenstone Mill then come to a traffic island. ❷

If you wish, visit the village of Shenstone if in need of refreshment at this point or possibly to look at the dominating hill top church viewed along the route from a distance, with its older redundant structure adjacent. The old quarter of the village is quite attractive and contains a couple of interesting old pubs. I have to say though that the village is more the size of a small town and the route up to the church etc. involves a fairly tortuous walk through residential areas after having first turned left at the island then cut right across the sports fields. My advice is, should you wish to explore Shenstone, go there in the car after the walk!

Take particular care over direction now. Find the best way across to the other side of the traffic island and enter the road opposite, which is called Pinfold Hill. However, do not go literally more than a few paces along Pinfold Hill before turning off right along a narrow track (known as Leppards Way) through a grassed area. You soon join and continue with Black Brook on your right as it twists and turns and eventually brings you out at a footbridge across it.

Cross the footbridge and proceed ahead to a fenced boundary in about 100 yards where you pass through two fence posts before continuing on a bearing half left on a well used path through a field towards a railway bridge. You will climb some steps before crossing the bridge and then walk along a broad track through a field. Bear left at a junction after a further 200 yards and stay on the track until reaching a short section of hedge line just before the track exits onto a lane. More directional concentration is required here. Do not continue to the lane – where the hedge line starts cut sharp right across and up the large adjacent field passing about 50 yards to the right of an electricity pylon aiming for the field corner ahead. If the field is planted or boggy you may feel more inclined to follow the edge around the other side of the pylon to reach the same point, where there is a stile.

Cross the stile and a track then another stile into a field and continue the line more or less forward cutting off the bottom left corner to find a stile in a sparse hawthorn hedge. Cross this and continue the line diagonally across a field to go over a waymarked stile in the opposite boundary to the right of farm buildings. Immediately cross a second stile then turn left through the second of two gates (the first leads into the farmyard) into a field at the rear. Cross the field diagonally to find a stile to the right of the bottom right corner 150 yards ahead and, having negotiated this, turn left onto the adjacent farm track which exits at a lane after 100 yards or so (not the driveway to private houses which you come to a little before that point).

Turn right along the lane – there is a footpath – which takes you under the A5 and, immediately after that, go left at a waymark up some steps and over a stile into a field. Walk along the bottom edge parallel with the A5 and cross a dilapidated stile in a boundary (at the time of writing this stile was impassable but there was a gap in the hedge 20 yards to the right which allowed me to continue ahead in the next field). In point of fact the correct line in this next field is to move out from the left boundary and aim to the left of a row of cream cottages on the far side which have been neatly renovated. Again, at the time of writing, the farmer had marked the path across but, if it is not clear, I suggest you keep to left hand hedge then turn right on reaching the field corner. You will find a stile to the left of the cottages – and to the right of Wall Village Hall – and you cross this to exit onto the lane leading back to the car park.

Leicestershire

5

Ashby-de-la-Zouch Castle and Staunton Harold

Maps: Landranger 128; Pathfinder 873 & 852; Explorer 245.
Start: From the car park in South Street Ashby-de-la-Zouch, which is located close to a driveway leading up to the castle. The castle is well signed from the town so you should not have difficulty finding it. Ashby itself is right on the border of Leicestershire and Derbyshire and is accessed via the M42/A42, exiting at the A50 Junction. GR 363165.
Distance: 9 miles.
Terrain: Generally easy going along well marked paths with no climbs of any significance. Starting with a trail through the town of Ashby-de-la-Zouch the way opens out into countryside to reach the splendidly located settlement of Staunton Harold, then returns via more farmland. A longish walk with a lot of interest so please allow plenty of time.
Refreshments: Plenty to be found in Ashby-de-la-Zouch plus cafés at Staunton Harold. There is also a pub en route at Heath End (The Saracens Head).

EH   Ashby-de-la-Zouch Castle

The town of Ashby-de-la-Zouch has its origins in Norman times when the Manor was granted to one of the followers of William the Conqueror. It later passed by marriage to the Zouch family, who were of Breton descent. The castle is now a substantial ruin, the earliest parts of which date to the twelfth century although there were major additions in the fifteenth century including Hastings Tower, the most impressive part of the remains.

William, Lord Hastings was Chamberlain to Edward 1V and was granted Ashby after the battle of Towton in 1461. His tenure did not last long as he was executed in 1483 by Richard III although his descendants occupied the castle until the Civil War, during which it withstood a long siege by Parliamentary forces before being surrendered and subsequently 'slighted'.

Open: 1 April to 30 Sept, 10 am to 6 pm; 1 to 31 Oct, 10 am to 5 pm; 1 Nov to 31 Mar, 10am to 4pm Wed-Sun. Closed 24-26 Dec, 1 Jan
Admission: £2.60/ £2.00/ £1.30. Inclusive of audio tour.
Tel: 01530 413343 .

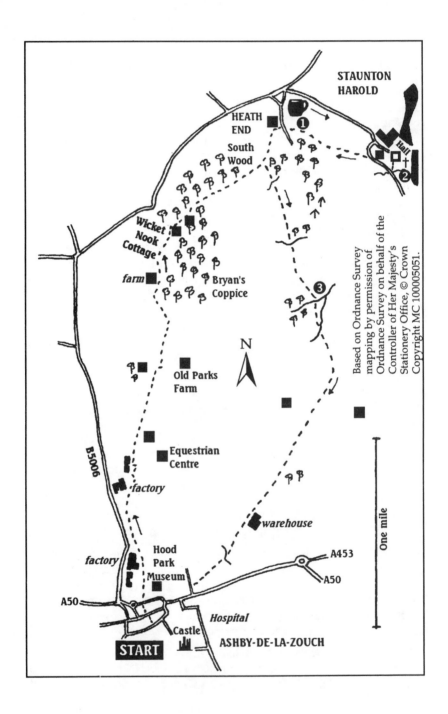

YOU CAN visit the castle at whichever end of the walk you like, although from the point of view of timing I would recommend that you do so at the start. Either way you will need to walk along the access drive and return to the road afterwards. Go down an alley directly opposite the car park and on emerging cross the main road diagonally left into Mill Lane to the left of Owen Jones Chemist. This will bring you out opposite another car park adjacent to the Museum/Library. Cross over the car park and on the other side enter Hood Park via a gateway. Keep to the tarmac path past the McVitie's factory and onto a narrower gravelly path which continues until you go through a kissing gate on the other side of a concreted access drive.

A grassy path now takes you towards and around the perimeter of another factory complex, after which you continue on a track to the right of an open meadow and alongside some residential properties and an equestrian centre. Cross the driveway to the equestrian centre onto a short path connecting with a tarmac driveway where you go forward in front of what appears to be a nursing home, beyond which the way proceeds to the right of a field. After crossing a boundary keep the same line in the next field where there are a pair of cottages in view to the half left. At the end of the field you meet a broad crossing stony track.

Ashby de la Zouch Castle

Cross the track directly and follow the right boundary of a field. The field edge shortly kinks right then left and after about a further 20 yds go through a gap in the field boundary and continue with a hedge on your left and within 100 yds a well walked path strikes off right to a waymarked stile in the adjacent boundary. Now go directly over a pasture field and through a waymarked gate in the opposite boundary. Good views are now opening up over countryside to the right. Follow the waymark ahead over the next field to another gate, with a farm complex over to the right – go through and turn right to gain a stile 100 yards ahead which takes you onto a broad farm track. Cross this then strike half left in the adjacent pasture field around to the rear of the buildings to go through a waymarked squeeze stile in a crossing boundary alongside the wood known as Bryan's Coppice.

You immediately go over another stile on the far side of a water trough and follow the top of an embankment in a curve around the wood then descend the slope to reach a public footpath sign positioned at a corner of the wood. From here continue ahead to a stile on the far boundary to the right of an oak tree. Cross into the next field following the left boundary until it kinks left after about 40 yards then stay more or less on the same line moving away from the boundary and aiming for a cottage on the far side. Cross a stile to pass to the left of it (Wicket Nook Cottage) and, after a few yards, you exit onto a tarmac driveway – do not go ahead following the waymark but turn right on the driveway towards another property. However, before reaching it, look carefully for a waymark on a post diverting you left to a stile at the rear of some outbuildings.

You will soon cross another stile after which bear right into a pasture field to follow the left boundary heading towards South Wood. At the end of the field cross another stile into the wood onto a broad grassy track, which may get boggy in the winter months. Ignore any side tracks and keep ahead at a waymark post but, after another 150 yards, ignore a broad track to your right and look very carefully for a narrow path also on your right leading to a gate and stile 30 yards further on at the edge of the wood. Cross and turn left now in a field following the edge of the wood and at the end of the field and the wood there is another stile to cross in a boundary hedge. In the next field go straight ahead to follow the boundary on your right before going left at a waymark in front of another wood.

Another 40 yards will bring you to a point where the wood boundary turns right but here you should only bear half right, effectively moving away from the wood crossing pasture field and aiming for a house visible ahead. The field is dotted with trees and you join a line of them before reaching the house and at the third tree, which is an ash, there is a waymark sending you right to another 30 yards ahead in front of some more trees. This takes you through onto a broad track leading out onto the driveway to the property. Turn left onto it (do not follow waymark over stile opposite) which takes you around to the right of the house and after another 150 yards or so you suddenly come across an isolated public house called the Saracens Head where you can, of course, take refreshment if you wish. In any event you need to cross in front of the pub to reach a junction with a road. ❶

You may have noticed some of the waymarks informing you that you have been walking along 'Ivanhoe Way'. Other indications, such as the names of buildings in the town of Ashby, suggest a connection with this fictional hero. The town was in fact well known to Sir Walter Scott, author of the novel 'Ivanhoe' which was published in 1819 and he chose Ashby as the venue for the famous tournament scene in the book. This led to a renewal of interest in the neglected castle and attracted patronage to the town. Clearly the current officials are still endeavouring to gain advantage for the area from the success of the novel, and who can blame them?

You do not actually go onto the road at all but turn sharp right along the lane signed Staunton Harold Church. This is a long straight lane which leads into the hamlet after about half a mile and on past the nurseries and craft centre and Staunton Harold Hall (now the Sue Ryder Foundation care home) down to the church in its attractive lakeside setting. ❷

On leaving go round to the left of the Hall up to a tall brick wall. Turn sharp left down a gravelled path alongside the wall then keep right at a fork to go over a footbridge leading out into the car park to the nurseries which you cross onto a lane and turn right. You will soon arrive at a waymark where the lane bends right and this directs you diagonally across a field to the top left corner where you cross a stile. If the field is planted you may

Staunton Harold Church NT

OWNED by the National Trust, the church and the adjoining Georgian hall were once part of an estate owned by the Shirley family, a long line of eccentrics one of whom was put to death in the Tower and another executed at Tyburn in 1760 for murdering his steward. The interior of the church is little changed from the seventeenth century and contains some splendid carved woodwork and box pews, a pre-Commonwealth organ and a rare type of wood framed clock.

Open 31 March to 30 September, daily except Mons & Tues. Oct, Sat & Sun. 1 to 5 pm. £1 donation requested.

wish to consider walking around the edge. Once in the next field following a course with a wood on your left, cross a stile in a boundary and continue along the edge of the wood before crossing another stile at the end. Turn right along the next field edge, and at the end you arrive at some stables. Immediately before stables cross a stile to the right of a metal gate and immediately pass through a wooden gate to right of the stables, then cross a stile onto a driveway in front of a house which you might recognize from the outward leg.

Retrace your steps again now by crossing the driveway directly and out over the tree dotted field to join the corner of a wood and turn left for about 30 yards to reach a waymark post in the field corner. Here we depart from the outward route by following the waymark direction ahead into the next field to the right of the wood. Continue ahead over a stile, followed quickly by a footbridge and another stile, to keep the line to the right of the next field boundary. Farm buildings are now in view ahead right and at the end of this field cross a gravelly track and stay on the same line in the next field. The farm on your right now is seen to be a large barn conversion. Negotiate a stile into an open field which you cross directly to the right edge of a small wood ahead.

Go along to the right of the wood through a gate and cross a footbridge, which at the time of my research was not in the best of condition! Once over continue ahead aiming for a wooden electricity pole on a brow then go under the wires to continue the line ahead and at the far side cross stiles on each side of a farm track. Go over the next field to another waymark about 120 yards ahead and in the next field proceed to the right of the boundary hedge to another marker post. Here cross a stile to the right of an oak tree and follow the field boundary down towards a wood in a hollow. Cross yet another stile on your right after only a few yards and go into the wood. Follow path as it climbs a bank and crosses a long footbridge across a deep gully. Continue ahead on a waymarked path for 20 yds to exit wood via another stile into a field. ❸

Follow the waymark ahead cutting off the left corner of the field to pick up the line of the wooded boundary on the left. On reaching the end cross a footbridge and continue ahead in the next field (which may be ploughed up or planted) and at end of this go through a waymarked gap turning right to immediately arrive at a crossing farm track. Go over this diagonally left and across a broad verge to a waymarked stile in the hedge. Cross the end of the field and pick up tree boundary on your left. Go through a gap in a crossing boundary with farm buildings over to the right then cross a stile after about 70 yards then yet another after a further 100 yards or so. Here there is a choice of routes and we go straight ahead onto a track between hedgerows.

You follow this track for some time as it works its way around the right of a small wood then alongside another large warehouse. When you arrive at the corner of the perimeter fence, leave the track to continue ahead over a waymarked double stile and stay ahead with a hedgerow on your right to the next waymark after 100 yards. Cross a stile into the next field now approaching Ashby and you come to a waymark and stile on your right together with a footbridge which you cross and bear left onto a narrow path between trees. This shortly exits right into a field which you cross diagonally cutting off the left corner, aiming towards the right of the end house in view. The way narrows up to a kissing gate which you go through before crossing the next field diagonally to the opposite corner at the rear of some houses.

Here there is a marker post sending you through a narrow gap in the hedge and along to the rear of the houses. At the end, go through another kissing gate and turn left onto a concrete driveway leading up to the main road. Turn right onto it and after about 120 yards take the first left signed Ashby District Hospital and after a further 100 yards, before the road loops left, turn off right through church precincts and exit via main gates. Turn left onto a lane and very shortly arrive back at the start.

6

Haughmond Abbey and Battlefield Church

Maps: Landranger 126; Pathfinder 869; Explorer 241.
Start: At Haughmond Abbey which is located about four miles north-east of Shrewsbury Town Centre just off the B5062. Approach from the east would be via the M54 and the Town's by-pass (A49) before turning right onto the B5062. GR 543153.
Distance: 5¼ miles or 8¼ miles.
Terrain: From the ruins of a twelfth century Abbey the walk traverses across Haughmond Hill with some magnificent views over Shrewsbury and beyond. There is a well worthwhile optional extension over farmland to visit the splendid redundant Battlefield Church, erected on the site of the Battle of Shrewsbury in 1403. No climbs of any significance.
NOTE: Please bear in mind that the Church is only open on Sundays in May-August between 2-5p.m. (although a key may be obtained at a nearby garage during normal business hours – see pages 36 and 39). It is, therefore, suggested that you look around the Abbey at the start rather than leaving it until after the walk.
Refreshments: There is a public house in Uffington (The Corbett Arms).

EH   Haughmond Abbey

HAUGHMOND ABBEY comprises the impressive remains of a twelfth century Augustinian Priory, built in the Early English Style, the highlight of which is probably the splendid three-arched entrance to the Chapter House, which retains its late medieval timber ceiling, and some fine medieval sculpture.

After the Dissolution part of the Abbey was transformed into a Tudor mansion but most traces of that are now gone while quite substantial parts of the Abbey remain, including the infirmary, refectory, kitchens, great hall and Abbot's lodging.

The Abbey was built hard up against the side of Haughmond Hill and some of the walls have lower courses hewn out of the natural rock. A brother house to Lilleshall, it was wealthy and highly respected – now its remains possess an atmosphere of great serenity and tranquillity.

Open: 1 April to 30 Sept, 10 am to 6 pm; 1 to 31 Oct, 10 am to 5 pm; Admission: £1.95/ £1.50/ £1.00.
Tel: 01743 709661.

RETURN to the road from the Abbey and turn left along it uphill for about 200 yards then bear right along another lane signed Upton Magna and Withington. You will shortly pass a quarry entrance and, after a further 150 yards or so, turn off right into Haughmond Hill car park. Keep left at the fork on entry to reach the information board describing various walk routes over the hill, then take the path about 15 yards to the right of it going into the wood (NOT the path leading off to the left!)

You very shortly join a broader track and pick up a waymark post with blue, red and yellow markers. When you come to a fork bear right along a narrower path where you drop the yellow marker and proceed through some pleasant, mainly deciduous, woodland. Eventually, the path curves left into a grassy clearing where there is another fork – keep right here on the blue path only and follow the blue markers for some time, through attrac-

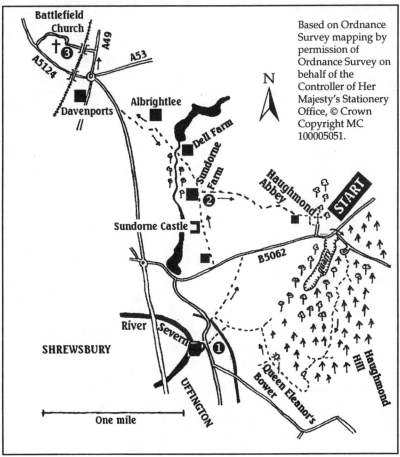

Based on Ordnance Survey mapping by permission of Ordnance Survey on behalf of the Controller of Her Majesty's Stationery Office, © Crown Copyright MC 100005051.

Haughmond Abbey

tive mixed woodland. When you arrive at a junction with a broad track turn left onto it then, after only 80 yards, bear right at the next blue marker down a flight of wooden steps and follow the path round into a picnic area.

On top of the rocky outcrop you get a superb view over Shrewsbury and the Severn Valley below. When ready to continue, keep following the path to the left and, on reaching a junction, bear right in a downward direction departing from the marker posts altogether. After a gradual descent the path hairpins right to continue downwards but around the base of the hill. Ignore a stile to the left after about a quarter of a mile. *Opposite this stile is the fir crowned knoll known as Queen Eleanor's Bower.*

Stay ahead on the path past a large outcrop on your right, on top of which is an old fort. You reach a point where the track veers sharp left through a belt of trees at right angles to the hill (if you continued straight on you would arrive back at the Abbey after about a mile) and enter on what can be a fairly muddy section which passes under an electricity pylon. What you do now depends upon whether you feel inclined to take refreshment at the Corbett Arms in Uffington. If not, continue ahead for 200 yards, keep right at a fork and immediately exit onto a farm track alongside a Forestry Commission notice and turn right.

If you do then, immediately after the pylon, branch off left along an indistinct grassy track and fork right to cross a fence stile between two horse chestnut trees and into a field towards the village. Cross the field directly aiming for an old bridge over a disused canal and, once over this, continue ahead in the next field with a hedge on your right to exit via a stile onto a farm track. After 100 yards you emerge onto a road in Uffington with the Corbett Arms in front of you. ❶

Leave the village by turning right in front of the Corbett Arms (or left on coming out of it!) and proceeding past the church. On the crown of the ensuing bend bear off right along a track to the gap and Forestry Commission sign referred to above. Go past this, or having turned right at this point if deciding not to visit Uffington, bear left at a waymark after 20 yards to come face to face to face with a gas station. Turn right in front of the compound onto a path between fencing and an embankment to a brook.

Cross a stile into a field and walk along the edge of it until reaching a waymark post after some 80 yards. There is a choice of

Queen Eleanor's Bower

LEGEND has it that this is where Eleanor, the queen of Henry IV, received the news of his victory at the battle of Shrewsbury in 1403. Also here is Douglas's Leap, although exactly where is a little uncertain. The 4th Earl of Douglas (Black Douglas) was a Percy ally who had in fact been captured by them at the border battle of Homildon Hill in 1402. He escaped here after the Battle of Shrewsbury but was captured when his horse fell. An official account by E. J. Priestley suggests that Douglas was wounded in the battle and captured. Hall's statement, in 1548, was that Douglas was captured after 'fallyng from the cragge of a mountagnie' a spot later identified as being on Haughmond Hill (Shakespeare's 'Yon Busky Hill' in *Henry IV Part 1*). There is no firm evidence of this – only folklore, but visit the atmospheric Battlefield Church to discover more about this important event in English history.

routes here and we need to continue round the field edge, cross another stile in a boundary fence then another 15 yards ahead in the right hand hedge just at the point where it turns left. You cross a further stile onto the B5062. Turn left, cross the road with care, and walk along it for about 300 yards until you arrive at a farm equipment warehouse on your right. Just before it cross a stile taking you to the left of a line of poplars.

The way crosses the line to continue to the right of the trees and along the edge of a sports field – the point of crossing is not critical. At the end of the sports field you go down a dip and a flight of steps then cross a brook and a stile to emerge into a pasture field. Bear slightly right across the field heading to the right of some unusual looking farm buildings ahead. Cross a stile by a gate in the field boundary and turn left on a tarmac driveway to reach Sundorne Castle Farm. You are met with the strange, extensive and largely abandoned remains of Sundorne Castle.

Once past the property continue on the tarmac driveway through a residential settlement and, after about 200 yards, you arrive at Sundorne Farm. ❷

On arrival at the crossroads by the farm you need to choose whether to go on up to Battlefield Church or short circuit back to Haughmond. I can without hesitation say that a visit to the former, which commemorates one of the most important battles in English history, will be well worthwhile (although you could, of course, cheat by going in the car afterwards!) and if you decide to go there please skip the next three paragraphs. Remember that

Sundorne Castle

THIS was home to the Corbett family and originally of Georgian origin but in the early nineteenth century it was completely remodelled and extended in fashionable Regency gothic (similar to others at Rowton, Apley Park and Quatford). It was a huge property and as opulent inside as it was out – a symbol of the gracious living of wealthy Victorians. You can perhaps visualise the scene on a summer afternoon with croquet being played in the magnificent gardens, others rowing on the nearby lake and carriages transporting visitors through the monumental castellated brick gatehouse which you walk by now. Sadly, or not – depending on your point of view – this relic of an extravagant bygone age was substantially demolished in 1955, the site of the main house now being marked by a silage bunker.

the Church is only open on Sundays in May-August between 2pm and 5pm – at any other time *during normal business hours* a key may be obtained from Davenports Hire Centre (tel: 01743 462950) – see page 39.

Those returning to Haughmond should turn right at the crossroads onto a concrete driveway and past some silage stores and a slurry pit, all of which was a little smelly on my visit! Follow the driveway almost to its end where there is a fork – take the right option through a waymarked gate into a field. Now bear slightly right away from the left boundary but not quite diagonally across the field and, as you approach the opposite boundary, you will see a stile about two thirds of the way along from the left corner. In fact there is a footbridge between two stiles and another choice of routes.

The way is ahead in the next field following the left boundary. You pass to the left of a fenced hollow to cross a stile in the opposite boundary and, in the next field, bear half right to cross a further stile and then a fence stile in the opposite boundary of the adjacent field. You have the Abbey as a back-drop now and continue the line more or less forward in the next field to the right corner aiming directly for it.

Crossing a stile here will bring you onto a muddy farm track and you turn left onto it towards the Abbey. Continue ahead to

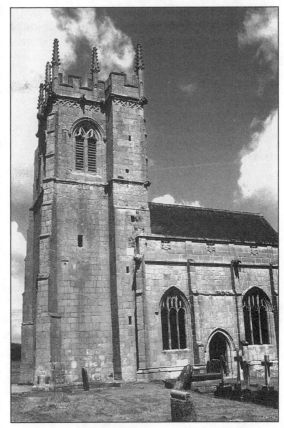

Battlefield Church

the left of a post & wire fence to reach a stile on the right just in front of the rear part of the Abbey precincts. This is a junction with the Shropshire Way, denoted by the buzzard waymark, and you cross the stile to follow the field boundary alongside the Abbey before crossing another stile at the end, after which bear left to a further stile which brings you back to the car park.

If taking the Battlefield extension you will need to memorise the outward route carefully in order to re-trace your steps back to this point. From the farm crossroads, go straight ahead but after

The Battle of Shrewsbury

The Battle of Shrewsbury on 21 July 1403 marked the end of the attempt by Henry Percy (Hotspur) to depose Henry IV and St. Mary Magdalene Church was built five years afterwards on the general site of the battle. It does not, however, mark the location of the early fighting, which probably took place on and around the low ridge to the north-west of the church. It was erected by Royal Charter to commemorate the King's victory and as a memorial to those who fell in the battle and were buried on the spot. Shakespeare's Henry IV part I contains a graphic account of the battle which resulted in Hotspur's death as well as up to 3000 men from each side.

Those well versed in the history of this period will recall that the Percy family had previously assisted Henry (then Bolingbroke) to the throne following the abdication of Richard II. Henry's reign provoked hostility from some English nobles and the Percys became aggrieved because of Henry's failure to repay them the cost of repelling the marauding Scots. The Percys forged an alliance with the Welsh leader Owain Glyndwr (Henry had also refused to pay the ransom of a member of the family who had been captured by Glyndwr), and the royal army made haste to put down the rebellion.

The magnificent, now redundant, church is atmospheric. Perhaps that is engendered by its vast emptiness but it is not difficult to imagine the remaining presence of those who fought and died near this spot. It fell into ruin after the dissolution of the monasteries under Henry VIII and, after restoration in 1862, was used as a Collegiate church. It has a beautifully tiled floor and stained glass windows depicting the twelve Apostles. The Coats of Arms of the various nobles taking part in the battle are displayed around the vaulted roof and there is a small exhibition about how the battle was fought and won.

only a few yards cross a waymarked stile on your left into a field. Once in the field with your back to the stile, bear half right aiming to the left of some farm buildings.which are just visible. You cross a stile onto a farm track and keep left, going away from the farm.

The track takes you downhill over a stream, after which bear right at a junction and you will shortly arrive at a stile into a field. Once over, continue the line more or less across and up the field towards the left corner of a walled garden around Albrightlee farmhouse. Continue around to the left of the garden and cross a stile onto the farm driveway. After only some 40 yards cross another stile on your left into a field which you traverse directly to a stile leading onto a grassy track. Turn left onto it but after a few yards look for a double trunk of an oak tree on your right with a fence stile across it. Having negotiated this and a subsequent stile into a field, follow the boundary on your left until crossing a further stile, then another after a few yards which takes you out onto the Shrewsbury by-pass. Turn right along it for a short distance to reach a traffic island.

If you need to pick up the key to Battlefield Abbey turn left towards the town centre and Davenports Hire Centre is on your right after 200 yards or so before reaching the Red Lion pub. Otherwise or afterwards, from the island, continue ahead along the A49 Whitchurch Road and, after about 250 yards turn left up a lane following a sign to the Church (you may see a Battle Heritage Site sign along the new A5124 off the island – ignore if you are walking as the route described above is better but if you are visiting by car this road may be the best option). ❸

On leaving the church, re-trace your steps back to the crossroads at Sundorne Farm. Turn left here and pick up the return route back to Haughmond as described above after point 2.

7

Boscobel and White Ladies

Maps: Landranger 127; Pathfinder 891; Explorer 242.

Start: From the car park at Boscobel House, Bishops Wood which is right on the border of Shropshire and Staffordshire (the walk actually straddles the two counties), some eight miles to the north-west of Wolverhampton. The approach from that direction is through Codsall but, from most other directions, the best way is probably via the A5 which runs about one mile to the north of Bishops Wood. GR 837083.

Distance: 6¼ miles.

Terrain: A pleasant walk through attractive countryside associated with the escape of Charles II from the Battle of Worcester. Some excellent views over easy to follow paths with nothing other than the gentlest of climbs.

Refreshments: The Boscobel House tearoom is open Tues-Sun during the summer only. There is a public House in Bishops Wood (The Royal Oak, what else!) where snacks and meals are available.

EH Boscobel House and White Ladies Priory

BOSCOBEL is a beautifully restored seventeenth century hunting lodge, famous for hiding Charles II from the forces of Cromwell following the King's defeat at the battle of Worcester in 1651.

There are few who have not heard the romantic story of the oak tree in whose branches Charles hid to avoid capture and his subsequent escape to Bristol disguised as a servant. A descendant of that same oak is still in the grounds and a fascinating tour around the house will bring alive the events surrounding this important piece of history and the characters involved.

Open: 1 April to 30 Sept, 10 am to 6 pm; 1 to 31 Oct, 10 am to 5 pm; 1 to 30 Nov, 10am to 4pm Wed-Sun; 1 to 31 Dec, 10 am to 4 pm Sat-Sun.
Admission: £4.30/ £3.20/ £2.20. Souvenir shop.
Tel. 01902 850244.

THE nearby White Ladies Priory was a large house built on the site of a medieval nunnery of the Cistercian Order and it was here where Charles was first taken after his flight from Worcester.

The house has long since gone but the remains of the nunnery church are preserved together with some interesting gravestones. The name 'White Ladies' refers to the pale colour of the undyed wool worn by the nuns as the information board on site reveals.

Admission free at any reasonable time.

FROM Boscobel House turn left along the lane signed White Ladies Priory and continue on it for about three quarters of a mile. As you walk along expansive views open up across the Shropshire countryside towards the Wrekin, one of the county's best known landmarks. After some 500 yards there is an excellent view of Boscobel House looking back.

Turn right at the sign to White Ladies Priory onto a well defined if sometimes muddy path to arrive at the Priory after 150 yards. After completing your visit return to the path and turn left onto it until reaching a wooden gate leading into a long narrow field. Go through it and continue ahead as the field rises, keeping close to the right side hedge. As you will now observe the waymarks denote 'The Monarch's Way' a trail which traces the

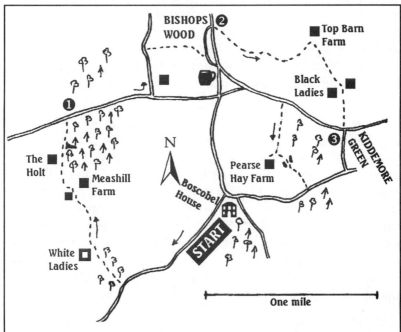

Based on Ordnance Survey mapping by permission of Ordnance Survey on behalf of the Controller of Her Majesty's Stationery Office, © Crown Copyright MC 100005051.

route taken by Charles II after the battle of Worcester. At the top of the field Meashill Farm comes into view and you pass through a small gate onto a path running alongside an orchard.

On reaching the farm buildings, go through a gate onto a concrete path but after only 10 yards you are obliged to turn right in front of a 'sleeper' fence before emerging in the stable yard. Cross the yard diagonally to the left corner and exit via a metal gate, after which bear right along a surfaced driveway leading away from the farm. Stay on this as it goes through an S-bend where you ignore a waymark left, as here we depart from the Monarch's Way which shoots off towards Tong, a village to the west through which Charles passed after staying at White Ladies in his abortive attempt to escape to Wales. The driveway continues past 'The Holt' and then Hawkshead Pool to reach a junction with a public lane. ❶

Turn right onto the lane and stay on it for roughly half a mile until, about 150 yards after passing White Oak Farm, you bear left along another lane. You cross the border into Staffordshire by Park Oak Farm on your right then pass a modern bungalow also on your right, after which the lane curves gently through an S bend. As you go through the second bend look carefully for a stile concealed in the hedge on your right about 15 yards after the second oak tree. Having negotiated this stile proceed ahead in a field following the left boundary where, on a clear day, you can enjoy distant views towards the Telecom Tower on Cannock Chase.

You are forced to clamber over an extremely awkward fence stile before continuing to follow the left field boundary and, almost at the end, cross a stile to continue directly ahead on a fenced path which emerges at a road junction in the village of Bishops Wood. If you require refreshment turn right then right again on reaching the 'main' road and the Royal Oak will be found on your right after a short distance. On leaving turn left and simply continue along the road to reach point 2. Otherwise, bear left at the junction referred to and walk through a residential estate. After a while the road narrows and loops right to join the 'main' road by a telephone kiosk. ❷

Cross the road directly (or turn right if coming from the Royal Oak direction) onto a sandy bridle path. Continue on this as it crosses a field then narrows to pass alongside an almost fortified cottage. The path gently descends between high hedges then emerges onto a stony drive before curving left and rising steadily to arrive at Top Barn Farm. Turn right in front of the house and follow the track as it passes to the right of the farm buildings then descends towards 'Black Ladies' which comes into view ahead.

The track passes between a converted cottage residence and a stable yard before bearing right along the front of the main house. Black Ladies is the most splendid Jacobean mansion of extensive proportions with wonderful architectural lines and was also a former priory. However, the foundation was Benedictine and therefore different to White Ladies – they had nothing to connect them except their proximity (even though they are in different counties) and a spirit of mutual rivalry. Another difference was the colour of the nun's habits and, as you may have guessed, those at Black Ladies were distinguished by garments of that hue, hence the name. Now continue along the driveway to the house (but going away from it) until you emerge onto Kiddemore Green Road where you turn right back towards Bishops Wood. ❸

You pass the Bishops Wood name sign and continue past a pair of semi-detached houses. After a further 150 yards, immediately before a 40 mph sign, branch off left by a cottage

Black Ladies

along a farm track leading to Pearse Hay Farm. On reaching a holly hedge directly in front of you do not turn right to the farm but go left through a wooden gate along a track which curves gently to the right as it crosses a field towards a wood. You are now back on a section of the Monarch's Way.

The track passes between two pools then rises to run alongside a field and emerge onto a narrow lane by Eva Cottage. Turn right along this lane and continue for just under half a mile to join the main road. Bear right here for about 200 yards to return to Boscobel House.

Boscobel House

8

Ancient Stones and Ancient Mines

Maps: Pathfinder 888, 909; Landranger 137; Explorer 216.
Start: The car park at Hope Village Hall. Hope is a small settlement just off the A488 about twelve miles south-west of Shrewsbury and nine miles north of Bishops Castle. From the Shrewsbury direction you proceed through Minsterley for about 4 miles and take a right turn in Hope and the Village Hall is located on the right after about a quarter of a mile. GR 340017.
Distance: 8¼ miles.
Terrain: A spectacular and mystical trail over superb hill country. Some climbs but nothing terribly difficult.
Refreshments: There is an excellent pub, The Stables Inn, at Hopesgate a short distance from the starting point and a village shop in Bentlawnt. There is also a pub on the A488 (The More Arms) a little over halfway round – see text.

FROM the car park turn right onto the lane and shortly turn left at a crossroads towards Bentlawnt. You continue on a gradual climb through the village and reach another crossroads where you proceed as if continuing ahead but bear immediately right down the waymarked driveway to Hope Park House. Do not be tempted to take another waymarked path a little further to your right. You leave the driveway almost straight away by crossing a stile on your left onto a grassy path through an enclosure which leads you between hedgerows to another stile in front of a field.

Cross the stile into the field with the boundary on your left, go over another stile in a crossing boundary and, at the end of the next field, cross a further stile onto a tarmac lane. Turn right here then go immediately left over a stile into a pasture field and head straight towards Brownlow Callow Hill with its botanically important grouping of Scots Pine on top. The trees are all that remain of a much larger Victorian plantation which was adopted in 1982 by the County Council. The hill is a source of legend and tales of witches.

You keep fairly tight on the base of a mound on your left and you will find a stile in the far boundary. Cross onto an indistinct path which gradually closes with a fence and dry stone wall

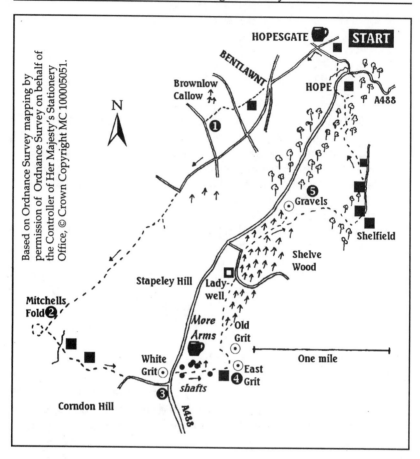

coming in from the left. Good views open up now to the right over Welsh border country and Corndon Hill, which you will get a little closer to later, over to your left. You join the dry stone wall at the top left corner of the field and cross a stile onto another lane. **1**

Turn left along the lane and after about a third of a mile bear right at a crossroads towards Hillgate and Stapeley Hill. At a point where the lane turns right after a further third of a mile continue ahead following Public Right of Way signs to negotiate a wooden barrier onto a stone forestry track. This rises and reaches a point where it bears left – however, you need to carry straight on here on a narrower waymarked track which curves right and continues to climb gently as it bears left alongside a post & wire fence. Ignore a waymark offering a left turn marked by a yellow arrow and instead follow the orange arrow ahead to reach a barred gate after a further 50 yards.

Go through the gate and proceed now on a clear grassy track through heathland with fantastic views over to the right towards Wales. You shortly continue ahead at a junction where a track comes in from the left, following which the path becomes a little more rocky. The outcrop of Stapeley Hill is now to your left and you fork left to follow the waymark posts for some time down to Mitchells Fold Stone Circle. This section marks the route of an ancient way along Stapeley Hill which has probably been in use since prehistoric times. ❷

When ready to depart, stand with your back to the tallest stone with the bulk of Corndon Hill to your half right. Now walk directly ahead on a broadish grassy track with a farmhouse in view. You are shortly joined by a post & wire fence on the left and the path develops into what can be a muddy track which descends to cross a stream via a sleeper bridge. You continue past the farm entrance and keep right at a fork where some further farm buildings are located off to the left. Note at this point the rocky crags of the Stiperstones in view ahead – another landscape steeped in folklore and tales of the devil!

Mitchells Fold

MITCHELLS FOLD is a desolate place with a mystical atmosphere and one of the most dramatic of Shropshire's many prehistoric monuments. It is estimated to be between 3200 and 4000 years old and comprised thirty stones, of which only fifteen are now visible. The circle was most likely to have been the focal point of ceremonial rituals for the local Bronze Age community and, when not used for such purpose, it may have served as a meeting place for trade. An information panel provides more data and also tells the legend of a magic cow, but I will leave you to read that for yourselves. Those particularly interested in archaeological sites of this type will have noted already earthworks in the form of linear banks running across the area. A continuation of the path out from the other side of the circle crosses over one of these banks which were apparently constructed to divide up the land into cultivated plots and may have been an early form of boundary. There are a number of other prehistoric sites on and around Stapeley Hill linked by paths which are easy to follow. Details are contained in a leaflet available from local tourist agencies and information centres or from Shropshire County Council.

Mitchells Fold

Lead Mining in Shropshire

T HE White Grit Pumping Station is the first of numerous relics of a once thriving industry which you will see on the second part of this walk. In 1872 the mines in this area produced 10% of the national output and brought great prosperity for a while, although this was fairly short lived due to the wildly fluctuating price of lead which resulted in many companies going bankrupt. By 1895 there was only the nearby Snailbeach mine left and even this closed in 1911.

The Grit mines have the longest history and their origins can be traced back to Roman times; indeed there is a whole area of opencast workings known as Roman Gravels which you will pass later on the route. Mining escalated from 1800 onwards and shafts were sunk deeply into the ore bearing rock. Pumping engines were necessary to drain the mines and these were built by Cornish engineers in characteristic style. They were enclosed in engine houses at various points in the network.

The history of mining in this part of Shropshire is a detailed and fascinating study and there are a number of publications on the subject for those wishing to discover more. I can but give a brief description of the main points of interest along the route of this walk

The track curves left and takes you well to the rear of these farm buildings and on past a couple of cottages, by which time the surface has changed to tarmac. You pass a further cottage where there is a waymarked gate and a cattle grid to cross. A few yards further on you join a lane and turn left onto it. A glance right here may reveal the sign for Powys – we are literally only a few yards from the Welsh border at this point. Continue on the lane until reaching a junction with the A488 and turn left. Notice on your left the remains of the engine house to White Grit mine. ❸

Cross the main road with care and, after 100 yards go over a stile on your right into an upward sloping field. (Before doing so, if the idea of refreshment appeals, the More Arms is situated 100 yards or so further along the main road.) *You walk up the slope to the right of several old shafts, some of which are not very adequately fenced off so please do not take any risks. You have been warned! Note the circular structure on your right – this is the former magazine house with its concentric outer walls for protection.* Cross a stile and continue upwards to walk to the right of a fir plantation to gain another stile, this time of the fence variety. The crags of the Stiperstones come into focus again here and there is evidence of a trial shaft on your right.

Cross the stile and continue forwards towards farm buildings ahead with more workings evident

Looking towards the Stiperstones

on your left. Aim for the left of the farmhouse to find a waymarked gate leading onto a broad stony farm track. This takes you to the left of the farm buildings and, directly opposite another farmhouse at the rear, take a left turn through the second gate on your left into a field. *Before doing so you can continue down the track to the remains of East Grit Mine and its imposing ruined engine house. The structure is clearly dangerous and should not be entered.* ❹

Once in the field proceed with the boundary hedge on your left and cross a stile into the next field where you stay on line towards another structure ahead. *On arrival you will see that this is quite a spectacular ruin and is in fact the former Old Grit Engine House and Mine. The Engine once installed here was bought from Boulton & Watt for £900 in the late eighteenth century. What a dramatic view from here across the East Grit ruins and surrounding workings. Imagine the noise of men and machines and the hard daily toil endured by the mine workers here at the zenith of production over 100 years ago.*

The path loops to the left of the mine to a stile by a gate. Cross this and proceed in a pasture field with a fence line on your left for about 100 yards until coming to another stile on level ground. There are terrific views left now past Corndon Hill into Wales. Cross the stile and turn right on a farm track heading towards a fir wood. After about 75 yards look half left across the adjacent field and there is a stile in a crossing boundary about 100 yards away. Make for that stile and cross it, ignoring a further stile some 40 yards further over to the left (if the field is planted you may prefer to walk around the edge).

In the next field continue the same line straight towards the left edge of the fir wood. Again, if the field is cropped it should be possible to work around the edge. At the corner of the wood go though a waymarked gate onto a broad farm track and proceed towards another structure ahead. Before reaching it you go through two gates onto a lane in front of another wood and turn left. *The structure is the remains of Ladywell mine and an example of commercial mining failure. A great deal of money was invested here during its short working life between 1871 and 1882 but only 835 tons of ore were extracted. Some restoration work has been carried out as you will see.*

From Ladywell continue along the lane and where it swings left after about 200 yards, bear right into Shelve Wood on a forestry track. You need the main one ahead, under a vehicle barrier, not the lesser path at right angles to it. After a while you emerge from the trees to be greeted by a magnificent view to the half left over the Shropshire Plain but, immediately adjacent, are part of Roman Gravels opencast mine. *As the name suggests operations here were started by the Romans but, much later, it was to become the most productive mine in the area after Snailbeach. There are in fact traces of some original Roman workings on the left in the wood just before you emerge from it. These opencast workings cover an extensive area sweeping right down to the A488 below and were closed then opened up again several times in the second half of the nineteenth century before being finally abandoned in 1894. If you venture onto the old workings please have regard to safety – at the time of my visit there was little in the way of fencing around what might be dangerous drops etc.*

Do not continue on the track past the workings. Directly opposite, and before the track narrows and drops more steeply, there is a fork right through the trees. Take this to shortly reach a waymarked gate. ❺

Go through the gate then strike ahead across open pasture with a fence over to your left and a hill to the right where you can see the remains of some quarrying. Towards the end of the field the right of way swings right to cut off the left corner and continue more or less at 90 degrees with the fence line still on your left. You go through a gate and descend into a wooded area with a farm below on the left. The path continues to drop and loops left towards the farm before which you go through another waymarked gate and continue ahead through the farm, passing firstly to the right of some open sided barns and then in front of the farmhouse. Follow the way through another gate onto a narrow tarmac lane.

This is a pleasant lane with attractive countryside on both sides. You go through another gate before another farm and about 15 yards further on bear left following the waymark between two properties on an upward path. Go through yet another gate and as you continue to climb panoramic views open up to your right over Snailbeach. After a steady climb the track levels out then peters out leaving you to continue ahead in a field alongside a post & wire fence. Just after you start to descend cross a stile on your right to continue downwards between trees. The path levels off briefly at the base of a hill on the right and here look for a gate and stile on your left just before the ground starts to rise again.

Go over the stile and stay on a downward course through trees and, on reaching a crossing track at the bottom, go through a waymarked gate into a sloping pasture field. Continue the line more or less straight forward cutting off the top right corner of the field to a stile 100 yards ahead in a tree line. Cross the stile into woodland on a path which can get overgrown with bracken in the summer. You negotiate a stile in a crossing boundary and go over a muddy section of ground. Now look carefully for a stile on your left into a field BEFORE reaching a gate into a farmyard. Once in the field follow the right boundary for 50 yards before crossing another stile on your right and walk the short distance across the farm driveway to reach the A488 again.

Turn right along the road (no footpath!) past a garage and, opposite Church Farm on your right, there is a waymark post and stile. Cross down some steps onto a path between fences which takes you over a footbridge and another stile and on to a rising path through trees around the rear of Hope Church. Unfortunately the church was locked at the time of my visit. The path continues an ascent to join a lane where you bear left to follow it back to the start point.

9

Acton Burnell Castle and Langley Chapel

Maps: Landranger 126; Pathfinder 889; Explorer 241.
Start:: From the car park at Acton Burnell Castle, a village situated some eight miles south of Shrewsbury. The best approach from that direction is via the A49 off which you turn left after Bayston Hill through Condover and continue on the lanes to Acton Burnell. The area is a maze of rural lanes and reference to a map would be advisable. From the south there is a turning right off the A49 through Longnor which will get you there or if travelling from the east you may prefer to take the lanes off the A458. GR 534018.
Distance: 6 miles.
Terrain: Easy walking along lanes and countryside in this pleasant corner of Shropshire. Some good views and gentle climbs only. Plenty of interest.
Refreshments: Nothing apart from a shop in Acton Burnell.

EH Acton Burnell Castle

ACTON BURNELL CASTLE is a ruined fortified manor house built in the late thirteenth century by Robert Burnell, Bishop of Bath & Wells and Chancellor of England. He was an influential man and a personal friend to King Edward I who, in 1283, summoned one of the first parliaments to be attended by the Commons as well as the Lords to meet at the Castle. This must have been an earlier structure as it is known that the ruins you can see now date from 1284.

There are information boards to tell you something of the Castle's fascinating history through to the mid seventeenth century, by which time most of it had been demolished. In the eighteenth century a new house, Acton Burnell Hall was built on the far side of the old Castle and this is now a college for overseas students.

Adjacent to the Castle is the church which was built by Robert Burnell at around the same time in the late thirteenth century, although it was substantially restored in the late nineteenth century and the present tower added. The building is of considerable architectural interest and contains a number of unusual artefacts and monuments, including a magnificent Elizabethan monument to

Richard Lee, to whom the Manor passed at that time. There is a
leaflet available for those wishing to obtain further information but
this says nothing about the ancient churchyard which I found to be a
strange and atmospheric place.

Entry to the Castle is free at any reasonable time.

WHEN ready to start the walk proceed down the entrance
drive back into Acton Burnell village and, at the
crossroads, turn right towards Shrewsbury. After
about quarter of a mile the houses end and you bear right along a
lane signed Kenley, Hughley and Cressage. You stay on this lane
for about one and a half miles but it it is quiet with pleasant views
over surrounding countryside and the Wrekin over to the left.
Ignore the turning left to Acton Pigot and pass the entrance to
'Sham Castle', secluded behind its high stone wall, before
continuing on the lane towards a large farmhouse. You ignore
another left turn before getting to it but, about 200 yards after
passing the farm (Evenwood) and just before another left turn,
bear right through a gate onto a broad farm track. ❶

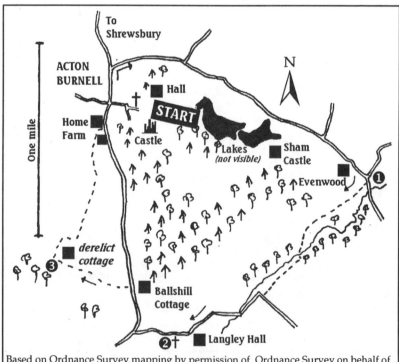

Based on Ordnance Survey mapping by permission of Ordnance Survey on behalf of
the Controller of Her Majesty's Stationery Office, © Crown Copyright MC 100005051.

54

You go through a gate in a crossing boundary by a stone barn and proceed into the next field. After a distance of perhaps 50 yards (not critical) you need to swing half left diagonally down the undulating field aiming for the far bottom corner by a brook. Once there you will find a rickety old gate and a bridge over the brook with another gate beyond. Having negotiated all this you come out into a field where you bear right with the tree line and the brook.

The boundary goes in and out a bit and the correct path is in fact a straight line, thus avoiding the indentations of the field edge. Which course you take will depend upon whether or not the field is planted but after a short distance you join a hedge line and continue with that on your right until exiting onto a lane via a stile. Turn right here and follow the lane round to pass the splendid Langley Hall with its mixture of styles and materials and, a little further on, you arrive at Langley Chapel on the left isolated in the middle of a field. ❷

On leaving the Chapel, stay on the lane and turn right at a junction after about a quarter of a mile. As the lane levels out there are some expansive views over to the left. You reach a pretty stone cottage on your right, called Ballshill Cottage, and immediately after it and opposite a stone driveway, take the gateway on your left into a field. The gate should have yellow marker tape on it. Keep to the right of a hedged boundary for about 120 yards before going through a gap in a crossing boundary and turning half right across the adjoining field to a point about halfway along the right boundary just to the left of an ash tree.

EH   **Langley Chapel**

As information panels inside the Chapel will tell you, this is a unique seventeenth century survival of the way Anglican churches were arranged at that time. There are box pews, a desk for musicians, bench seats around a communion table and an atmosphere which conjures up the strict religious code prevalent during the Civil War. It was abandoned in the last century as the local population had shrunk to below the level which could sustain the church and it was one of the first historic buildings to be rescued by being taken into the care of the State.

Entry is free at any reasonable time.

Langley Chapel

Here there is a gate to go through after which continue the line over the next field cutting off the left corner to a gate about 100 yards ahead in the corner. Go through into another field and walk along the edge with a post & wire boundary on your right. After some 100 yards go through the second of two gates on your right (waymarked). With your back to the gate turn left at an angle of about 30 degrees diagonally across a field aiming about 50 yards to the left of a derelict building. Before getting there you will reach a fence stile by a gate. ❸

Cross the stile and continue forward for a 40 yards before turning right to a waymark post to walk past the derelict building and then stay on the same line to a gate in the right corner of the field. Pass through the gate and turn right along a stony track with a hedge on your right. At the end of this field bear left keeping the hedge on your right to reach a gate in a crossing boundary and, once through, continue forward on a track to the left of a post & wire fence. This is a large field and as you go along, those of you with binoculars might like to have a look at the landmarks visible ahead and to the left. Almost ahead the monuments and spires of Shrewsbury pop out from behind the ridges around Bayston Hill and, following round to the left, Breiddon Hill topped with Rodney's pillar is clearly visible.

Further left can be seen the crags of Stiperstones then the impressive peaks of The Lawley and, behind, Caer Caradoc.

At the end of the field go through a metal gate onto a stony track which takes you across the next field for about 100 yards before you are obliged to go through another gate. Once in the adjoining field stay ahead on the stony track until you arrive at Home Farm. Now the correct right of way is along a right turn and through a series of farm gates but, in practice, walkers continue on for a short while then take the next available right turn to the north of the main building and out onto a lane almost opposite the farmhouse. Now turn left into Acton Burnell then go right in the centre to return to the castle.

Acton Burnell Castle

Shropshire

10

Wenlock Priory

> **Maps:** Pathfinder 890, 911; Landranger 127; Explorer 217, 242.
> **Start:** The Priory car park is well signposted and easy to find once you are in Much Wenlock. The town is situated on the A458 between Shrewsbury and Bridgnorth. It can also be reached from the north via Telford and the M54. GR 625002.
> **Distance:** 3 miles.
> **Terrain:** Mainly well used paths taking you up onto Wenlock Edge where there are super views over Much Wenlock and the Severn Valley to the north, then return via undulating farmland. A little climbing but nothing too strenuous.
> **Refreshments:** There are plenty of facilities in Much Wenlock.

EH   Wenlock Priory

THE atmospheric remains of Wenlock Priory recall much of the turbulence of early English history. Although largely rebuilt in the eleventh and twelfth centuries, the original monastery was founded in the seventh century after St Milburgha, daughter of a Mercian King and who was an early Abbess there. It was sacked by Danes at the end of the ninth century, refounded around 1080 by Roger de Montgomery, a Norman knight and survived until the dissolution of the monasteries by Henry VIII. Most of the buildings seen today date from the eleventh century although the ruins of a fifteenth century priors lodging also survive.

The town of Much Wenlock is steeped in history and a little exploration around its ancient streets will reveal a wealth of interesting buildings and architecture through the ages. We will pass a few of these on our return from the walk and, for those wishing to know more, leaflets are available from the Tourist Information Office.

Open: 1 April to 30 Sept, 10 am to 6 pm; 1 to 31 Oct, 10 am to 5 pm; 1 Nov to 31 Mar, 10am to 1pm, 2pm to 4pm Wed-Sun.
Admission: £2.70/ £2.00/ £1.40. Inclusive audio tour giving a unique insight into the buildings as well as those who worked and worshipped here.
Tel: 01952 727466.

WITH your back to the Priory turn right and walk along a quiet lane for about a third of a mile to a point where it bears sharp right in front of a small clearing. Here branch off left following a waymark along a path which shortly descends via steps onto a dismantled railway line, a former branch of the GWR running between Wellington and Craven Arms. Cross it diagonally up more steps opposite and at the top is a complex junction of paths. Continue ahead on a virtual straight line on the second path from the left. There is a quarry spoil heap to the right and after a few yards you turn right at a junction onto the Jack Mytton Way. For those not well versed in Shropshire folklore, Jack Mytton was an eccentric character who lived in the early part of the last century and known as 'Mad Jack'. Renowned for practical jokes he turned to drink and got into debt, was thrown into debtors prison and died penniless in his late thirties. This path takes you along the rear of a school and exits via a gate onto the A4169. ❶

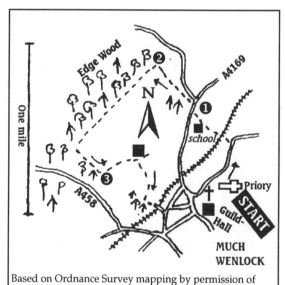

Based on Ordnance Survey mapping by permission of Ordnance Survey on behalf of the Controller of Her Majesty's Stationery Office, © Crown Copyright MC 100005051.

You may have spotted a ruined windmill on the rise to your right which you can visit although there is not a great deal to see. Turn right along the main road – there is a footpath – and after 80 yards cross carefully to go left through a waymarked gate into a field. Cross the field directly keeping parallel with a wood on your left and go over a stile in a crossing boundary to continue forward to the left of hedge. There are good views to the right to the Wrekin, the highest point in this part of the county, and you can also see the cooling towers of

Wenlock Edge

WENLOCK EDGE was formed about 420 million years ago during the Silurian period in a tropical sea and stretches in an unbroken line for fifteen miles between Benthall Edge above the Severn Gorge to Craven Arms. Since founding of the Priory pilgrims and others have trodden the way along it into the town. The underlying rock is limestone built up from the skeletons and shells of sea creatures, and subsequent earth movements created its present shape, tilting the rock strata gently down to the south-east. The limestone rock has been a valuable resource for building stone and as a flux in iron smelting. Even today it is quarried for aggregate.

Ironbridge Power Station. At a break in the hedge line curve left then right on a well defined path to pick up the hedge again but now to the right of it and stay on line until reaching the front end of Edge Wood, the extreme north-eastern extremity of Wenlock Edge. Cross a stile into the wood. ❷

Do not take the path to the right downhill but climb a short embankment to follow the path to the left of the wood. It rises to a boundary where there is a gap to go through before continuing ahead and through another gap in the next crossing boundary. Stay on course along the wood edge and through a further hedge boundary (ignoring a waymarked path on the left) and the next to yet another where there is a waymarked stump on the right at a convergence of paths. At this point turn left to follow the right hand side of the hedge heading towards the left of a small wood. Enter the wood keeping the same line and after a short distance transfer to the left side of the hedge along a field boundary. ❸

The way curves left and continues along the bottom edge of the same field. Go through a gap in a crossing boundary and continue towards a cottage in view ahead. At the end of this field is a choice of routes – take the right option through a metal gate into the adjacent field to walk along the left hedged boundary towards the left side of another small wood. You may note that we are on the Jack Mytton Way again. At the end of the field the path weaves into the wood and, on exiting, bear left onto a broad track down towards Much Wenlock. On reaching a tarmac surface go straight ahead over a bridge, past an agricultural yard and at a junction with a road bear left. After 120 yards turn right following the sign to Wenlock Priory. The second turning on the right, St Owens Road, will bring you to a junction with High Street where you turn right.

Now look on your left for a number of historic buildings. They are, in order, Raynalds Mansion – a seventeenth century facade to a medieval hall, The Corn Exchange opened in 1854 and now partly used as a library and, on the corner with Wilmore Street, The Museum which also houses the Tourist Information Centre. Opposite is the splendid Guildhall which was built in 1540 and until recently used as a Courtroom.

Turn left in front of the Guildhall and you pass by Holy Trinity Church before turning right into the Bull Ring. Here you pass on the right Priory Hall built in 1848 as a National School and now a local meeting place. The Bull Ring of course gets its name from the practice of bull baiting carried on there until the early part of the last century. A short distance will bring you back to the Priory car park.

The Guildhall, Much Wenlock

11

Clun Castle and Bury Ditches Hill Fort

> **Maps:** Landranger 137; Pathfinder 930; Explorer 201.
> **Start:** Anywhere convenient in Clun (there are two car parks, one quite close to the castle). The town is situated in a remote area of south-west Shropshire on the A488 about six miles equidistant between Bishops Castle and Knighton. GR 302809. As an alternative you could start from Bury Ditches Hill Fort (there is a car park) and take a break for refreshment in Clun. To find Bury Ditches take the lane out to the north from Clunton, which is on the B4368, three miles east of Clun, and follow it for a little over two miles. GR 325836.
> **Distance:** 7¼ miles.
> **Terrain:** A trail through part of the county's beautiful hill country, the epitome of Shropshire at its best, around an ancient hill fort and return to the town of Clun – all totally unspoilt by the 20th century. Some fairly stiff climbing is required, particularly up to the hill fort.
> **Refreshments:** There are three pubs and a café in Clun.

EH Clun Castle

THE fascinating town of Clun can trace its origins back to the Neolithic Period as artefacts held in the museum (located within the Town Hall) will verify. More recently, the Normans occupied the area and created the grid pattern of streets which is clearly evident. It takes its name from the river Clun over which there still spans a fourteenth century bridge, but its foundations were really laid in the seventeenth century when Henry Howard, Earl of Northampton was Lord of the Manor. He was the brother of the Duke of Norfolk executed by Queen Elizabeth for plotting with Mary Queen of Scots and founded the almshouses and Trinity Hospital in 1614.

The chapel and gardens of the hospital are open to the public and worth a short diversion to visit. In the nineteenth century the town was sustained by numerous cottage industries, including chair-making (exhibits of which can be seen in the museum) and at that time supported no less than fourteen pubs and alehouses!

The Castle is now a ruin and entry at any reasonable time is free. There are display panels to guide you through its history but, briefly, it was the border stronghold of Robert de Say in the eleventh century (he in fact held several manors in Shropshire as identified by some of their names, e.g. Hopesay and Stokesay) and was burnt in 1196 by Welsh rebels under Prince Llewelyn and again around 1400 by Owain Glendwr.It passed through the Fitzalan family up to the end of the sixteenth century when it came into possession of the Howards – see above – and sold in 1677 to the Walcots of nearby Walcot Hall. They in turn sold it to Lord Clive of India (who lived at Walcot) but, in the late nineteenth century, it passed back to the Howards who own it to this day. The last inhabitant was reputedly a Canada Goose which raised a family on top of the highest tower for three consecutive years in the mid-1970s!

Entry free at any reasonable time.

WHEN ready to proceed with the walk take the lane through the town opposite the Castle entrance (Newport Street) and you will come to a junction where you take the lane to the left going away from the town. Trinity Hospital is just down the right turn should you wish to visit it. You go past a sports field and Memorial Hall and after a total distance of about half a mile on this lane take what is effectively the first turning right off it down a stony farm track. This track shortly veers sharp left and continues alongside a stream. You soon cross a footbridge over the stream and start to climb.

The track continues upwards and sometimes muddily between high embankments. After quite a long climb you reach a waymarked gate – go through this and another after climbing along a field edge then stay on the same course towards a tree line ahead. As the ground levels out pause for a breather and admire the view backwards over the hills around Clun. You go through a further gate leading into Radnor Wood and follow a path around the left edge of it. The path descends through mixed woodland and at the bottom you bear left through a waymarked gate then immediately right in a field to another gate after about 120 yards. Go through then walk roughly half left across the field to a footbridge over a stream which you should be able to spot 120 yards below. Once over continue forward across another field to reach a broad crossing track running around the base of Stepple Knoll and turn right onto it at the waymark. ❶

On arrival at Stepple Farm cross a stile by a gate and continue directly ahead between farm buildings. Once past them bear left at a T-junction onto a broad farm track. After 250 yards cross a stile and stay on the track as it swings left then right to cross another stile with two waymarks. Take the lower one which keeps to the main track and you shortly arrive at another farmhouse. At a waymarked gate in front of it take the path left alongside the house (do not go through the gate!) to cross a stream. There is no footbridge and the ground can get muddy.

Now turn right to cross the centre of a sloping pasture field to a gate in the far boundary. Go through and continue the same line in the next field to go through another gate heading towards a small farmhouse in view. Go through yet a further gate to the right of the farmhouse, then ahead on a broad farm track and stay on it until exiting onto a lane. Turn left and after another 250 yards or so left again into the car park at the base of Bury Ditches.

As you will observe there are various designated ways spanning out from here including the Shropshire Way and Wild Edric's

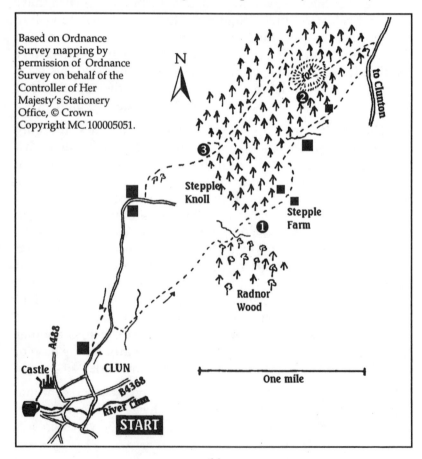

Based on Ordnance Survey mapping by permission of Ordnance Survey on behalf of the Controller of Her Majesty's Stationery Office, © Crown Copyright MC.100005051.

N

to Clunton

Stepple Knoll

Stepple Farm

Radnor Wood

A488

Castle

CLUN

B4368

River Clun

START

One mile

Way. Wild Edric was a legendary character who led local resistance to the Norman invasion. Eventually he came to terms with William, much to the distaste of his followers, and was banished. His death was never recorded and many legends grew up around him. Whenever his ghostly form is seen galloping furiously over the hills it is said to be a portent of war. Any sightings should be reported immediately to the authorities!

The routes are colour coded and we need to follow the path uphill to the right with red/green/blue markers. This is a long, fairly steep climb through pine woods. Almost at the top is a gateway and plaque giving some basic facts about Bury Ditches Hill Fort and you then pass through the original entrance to the fort itself. ❷

Clun Castle

Apparently there are over 20,000 ancient hill forts in the British Isles and this is one of the best of them. The plaque will give you some details which I will not repeat here except to say that this was a major settlement in the first millennium BC and the magnificent defences are still clearly visible. If you bear half right after the entrance you reach a viewpoint with superb 360 degree views through the Long Mynd, Ludlow, Clun, Offa's Dyke, Stiperstones and various other landmarks – on a clear day that is.

Continue on the track running along the top of the fort to exit over a stile, after which the track loops right and carries on for about quarter of a mile to reach a junction with the Shropshire and Wild Edric Ways. Turn left here and after about 120 yards the red route goes left but we stay ahead with the green route. The way descends gradually and at the bottom is a complex junction. You need to turn right, although effectively continue ahead, still following the green route. Ignore a track left where the main route starts to descend more steeply but, after another 30 yards, bear left where the main route curves right. You are now on the Jack Mytton Way and shortly exit the wood and go round a metal gate onto a broad track between hedgerows. **3**

Jack Mytton was an eccentric Shropshire character who lived in the early part of the last century and known as 'Mad Jack'. Renowned for practical jokes he turned to drink and got into debt, was put in debtors prison and died penniless in his late thirties. Stay on the track as it descends and swings left round a small wood to arrive at a junction by a stone cottage. Bear right on a heading towards farm buildings, pass between the farm buildings and continue the gradual descent on a tarmac lane, still on the Shropshire Way.

Look for a waymarked stile on the right after about half a mile from the farm. Cross and follow the waymark diagonally over a field (there is a little stream on the field side of the stile and the ground around it can be squidgy!) and go through a gap in a crossing boundary to another stile 30 yards ahead. Cross this and the next field aiming to the left of a cottage ahead where there is another stile to cross before turning left to follow a path around the boundary to join a broad track going downhill for 100 yards to rejoin the lane.

Turn right on the lane and continue past the Memorial Hall back into Clun.

12

Stokesay

Maps: Pathfinder 931; Landranger 137; Explorer 217.
Start: Car park to Stokesay Castle which is just off the A49, three quarters of a mile south of Craven Arms. GR 435817.
Distance: 5 miles.
Terrain: Undulating countryside with some excellent views across the Onny Valley. Mainly easy to follow paths but some parts muddy at times. A long ascent to Norton Camp but well worth the effort.
Refreshments: There is a tea room at the Castle and another adjacent to the car park. Otherwise there are plenty of facilities in Craven Arms.

EH ## Stokesay Castle

Stokesay Castle is a remarkably well preserved fortified manor house dating from the thirteenth century, strategically located close to the border with Wales. The seventeenth century gatehouse must be one of the most photographed in the land and there are numerous other aspects, architectural and historical, to delight the visitor. The Great Hall, for example, is almost untouched from its days of opulent medieval banquets.

Open: 1 April to 30 Sept, 10 am to 6 pm; 1 to 31 Oct, 10 am to 5 pm; 1 Nov to 31 Mar, 10am to 1pm, 2pm to 4pm Wed-Sun. Closed 24-26 Dec, 1 Jan
Admission: £3.50/ £2.60/ £1.80. Inclusive of audio tour, which is excellent.
Tel: 01588 672554.

IF time permits, visit the Church of St. John the Baptist, the churchyard of which extends almost up to the castle walls. Together with the castle the Church was once the focal point of a village community which has long since disappeared, leaving the Church isolated. The structure was rebuilt in the mid seventeenth century following damage in the Civil War and contains some fine woodwork of that period.

START the walk by turning right down the lane alongside the Castle. Continue past a pool, ignoring a Shropshire Way marker on the right, and before coming to a farm bear right through a gate onto a broad waymarked track with the pool on

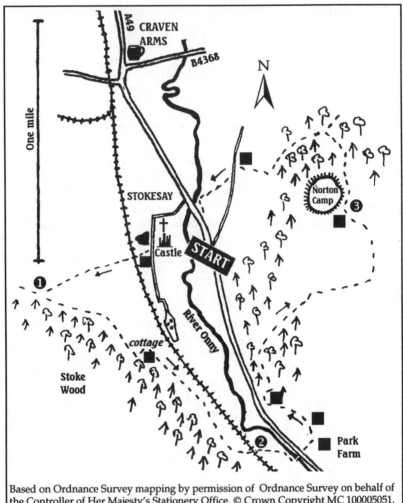

Based on Ordnance Survey mapping by permission of Ordnance Survey on behalf of the Controller of Her Majesty's Stationery Office, © Crown Copyright MC 100005051.

your right. After 100 yards you cross a rail line via stiles on each side and continue along the track passing to the right of a newish barn, to shortly go through a gate into a pasture field. Once in the field bear very slightly right to a waymarked stile on the opposite boundary – there is a faint track across to guide you in the right direction. Cross the stile and continue the same line forward over the next field to cross a stile on the opposite boundary before heading towards a wood, still on roughly the same bearing. Here there is a stile in the tree line and a look back from this point will be rewarded with a superb view of the Castle and surrounding countryside. **❶**

Cross the stile but after only 15 yards bear left onto a broader track. This winds attractively (and sometimes muddily) along the bottom edge of Stoke Wood although it can get a little overgrown in summer. Keep left at a junction and a little later ignore a waymark post and stile on your left. Eventually, you cross a stile by a gate and continue on the track as it descends gradually to reach a crossing track after about 80 yards. From this point you should be able to see Stoke Wood Cottage across the field opposite.

Do not be tempted to go through the wicket gate into the field but turn left and after 100 yards or so cross the front of the driveway to Stoke Wood Cottage and go over a stile into the field. The delightful prospect of a sewage works opens up below but, you will be relieved to hear, do not follow the waymark directing you that way but bear right across rough pasture to the right of a disused quarry, to a stile in a crossing boundary after 300 yards. Cross this and stay on line in the next field walking about 40 yards parallel to the right of the railway line to join a broad grassy track along the top of the embankment to the railway line.

You pass a pair of what look like old shelters constructed of local stone (remnants of former quarrying activity in the area?) and emerge into a field departing slightly from the left boundary fence to a stile in a crossing boundary about 120 yards ahead. You may note the Shropshire Way marker here and can see the River Onny below winding its way through the valley. Cross the stile and the next field to another stile in another crossing boundary. The waymark on this stile is confusing as it sends you left but the bearing is only slightly left to the bottom left corner where it meets the embankment to the railway line. There is a stile in the corner and also some gates. The objective now is to turn left under the railway bridge to emerge into a field and, depending upon whether the gate is in the closed position, you may or may not have to cross the stile to do it. **2**

The official direction is now diagonally right across the field to reach a point just to the left of a bridge over the river which you may be able to see in a gap in the tree line. However, the field is frequently planted and, if so, you might wish to consider taking the broad track straight ahead which then swings right alongside the river to the same point. On reaching the bridge, cross it to arrive at a junction with the A49.

Stokesay Castle

Cross the main road directly up the drive to Park Farm (there is a waymark to the left of the entrance) and at the top swing left across a farmyard to the left of some barns and to the right of another onto a broad rising track. Almost at the top of the rise where the track forks, bear left in front of a stone cottage and stay on the track, which shortly becomes metalled, going back downhill. It becomes stony again and continues the descent passing to the left of a neat cottage, shortly after which is a waymark post in front of the entrance to Keepers Cottage. Bear right here along a grassy track rising again and after 80 yards you reach a broad crossing track and turn right onto it.

The ascent is continued alongside a new plantation on a track which is most inappropriately named 'Rotting Lane' and swings left to reach a fork where you keep left to continue the climb. As the ground starts to level off a little and just before the new plantation ends, fork right along a narrower path to maintain the upwards direction. As the trees end on the left you are presented with another choice; again keep right following the blue marker post then go through a gate and into a large pasture field.

Walk along the right edge of the field to a point where the trees end on the right and cross a stile to continue the line forward but now to the right of a hedge. There are good views to the right – on a clear day you can see as far as the Malverns. Where you reach a gate onto a farm track, go through then turn 90 degrees left onto a broad track along another edge of the field you were previously in and with a hedge on your right. At the top go through another gate to stay on the track as it swings left. You shortly go under an arbour of holly and laurel to emerge by some derelict buildings and you proceed to the rear of the one in front to come face to face with the enclosure of the Iron Age Fort of Norton Camp. **❸**

It is likely that Norton Camp was strategically located to command wide views over this section of borderland and the major junction of ways around Craven Arms. Its sheer size suggests that it was a fortification of some importance and, together with Caynham Camp near Ludlow, was probably one of an interconnected chain of similar stations.

Unfortunately you are not able to enter the arena and must retreat to the derelict buildings and turn left to follow a well used path around the perimeter of the Camp. After a while there is another opening on the left providing a further view of the Camp. Continue on the main track along this very pleasant route and you shortly come to a waymark post where you fork right away from the Camp and to the right of a pheasant rearing

The seventeenth century gatehouse at Stokesay Castle

enclosure. You descend through attractive woodland to a waymark post where you effectively continue ahead.

At the bottom of the descent there is a waymarked stile on your right. Don't cross but continue on the path which runs along the bottom edge of Norton Camp Wood, and if you look right, there are expansive views over open countryside and towards Craven Arms. On a clear day you can see Long Mynd and Wenlock Edge beyond.

After another 200 yards or so the path loops to the right and changes to a sunken track before passing a Tudor style property to emerge onto a lane.

Turn left onto the lane. There are the curious remains of a former chimney piece in the field on your left and after 100 yards look for a waymark and stile on the right. Cross into a field from where you can see Stokesay Castle again. You can also see an electricity pole to the left of a belt of trees below and your way is diagonally across and down the field aiming about 20 yards to the right of it where there is a stile. If the field is planted you may prefer to walk around the edge. The River Onny also comes into the picture again and you cross the stile and then another stile after about 60 yards in the corner alongside the river.

From here walk the short distance across the bottom of the field you have just exited (this is one of those seemingly illogical routes which were created many years ago when the field boundaries and land topography were entirely different from today) and at the end turn left for 20 yards to cross a stile on the right up some steps to a lane, which is no longer used and blocked off to the right. However, you need to turn left and cross a stile by a gate to arrive at the A49 again. Turn right but cross the road carefully to a footpath on the other side. After 200 yards turn left into a lane which will take you back to the start.

13

Croft Castle and Mortimers Cross

Maps: Landranger 137; Pathfinder 972; Explorer 203.
Start: From the car park at Croft Castle. Access is available at most times but there is a charge. To get there you need to take the B4362 at Woofferton, which is on the A49 roughly halfway between Ludlow and Leominster, and follow it through for about five miles before turning right up the driveway to Croft (opposite the turning to Yarpole village). It can also be approached from the west via the A4110 from Mortimers Cross. GR 450656.
Distance: 7 miles.
Terrain: A wander through the picturesque Croft Castle Estate and across Croft Ambrey Fort with its magnificent views, followed by a descent to the scene of a fifteenth century battle and return via farmland. A splendid walk with lots of interest! *In fact there is so much that timing is more critical that on some walks if you want to see everything fully. My suggestion is that you do not leave it much later than 10.30 to start and aim to depart Mortimers Cross by 3pm. This should allow you to get back in time to look around the Castle before it closes.*
Refreshments: Mortimers Cross public house only. A welcome stopping place serving meals. There is a tea room at Croft Castle.

Croft Castle   NT

Croft is a Welsh border castle of considerable stature. Although the Croft family can trace its ownership back to Norman times, the present structure dates from the fifteenth and sixteenth centuries and has a basically defensive character which bears witness to the turbulent past of the Marcher lands.

The interior was re-fashioned in the eighteenth century during a break in the ownership of the Croft family; they returned to the property in 1923 and remain there to this day even though it is now in the care of The National Trust.

The Croft Estate covers 1563 acres comprising a mixture of woodland, pasture and parkland as well as an Iron Age hill fort. The woodland is actively managed to maintain the delicate balance between conservation and recreation and contains some notable species and attractive landscaping.

Open (2001): 31 March to 29 April: Sat, Sun and bank hol Mon.
2 May to 30 Sept: daily except Mon & Tues but open bank hol Mons.
6 Oct to 4 Nov: Sat & Sun. 1 to 5 pm.
Entrance fee to castle and grounds: £3.90, family £10. Grounds only
(open all year) £2.00 per car.
Tel: 01568 780246.

F ROM the car park walk back down the entrance drive and after crossing a cattle grid turn left down a waymarked track into woodland. You shortly bear left again on reaching a junction with a broader track in Fishpool Valley and here enter onto 'Mortimers Trail', a 30 mile way between Ludlow and Kington named after the powerful feudal family who owned considerable lands in this area.

Fishpool Valley is a Site of Special Scientific interest because of its seclusion, rich bird life and varied habitats. It comprises a series of

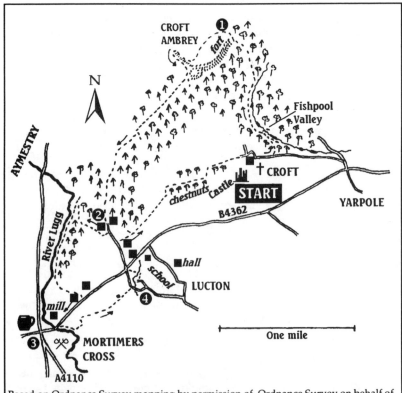

Fishpool Valley

*pools created in the late eighteenth century by two neighbouring
squires to further the Picturesque Movement – a reaction against
Capability Brown. The pool reached shortly comes complete with a
Grade II listed pump-house, built around the turn of the
nineteenth century to pump water to a nearby reservoir. There are
plans to restore it.*

Keep ahead at a junction by the pool going to the left of it
before embarking on a gentle climb through a valley. You reach
another junction of tracks in a small clearing and bear slightly left
to continue the climb on a narrower path following the
waymarked red route. Keep to the red route over a crossing track
and a further 100 yards will bring you to another broad track
which you cross diagonally to stay on Mortimers Trail along the
way signed 'Kington 20' – information I'm sure you will be
incredibly relieved to know!

The climb now becomes a little steeper and, on reaching level
ground, go through a gate and bear left to continue on Mortimers
Trail. After only some 50 yards, under a large Hornbeam tree and
before arriving at a gate, you will find a stile. Cross and proceed
along the path up to Croft Ambrey walking along the right edge
of the plateau and, perhaps, take a breather after what was quite
a strenuous climb. ❶

This is a large fourth century BC Iron Age hill fort almost 1000 feet above sea level with well preserved ramparts. It was built by Celtic warrior farmers and has commanding views over a wide expanse of country. You can see well into Wales on a clear day. The fort was abandoned as a defensive position by the Romans around AD50. There is a small exhibition in the castle which will provide more information for those interested.

As you walk along there are views to the right over the village of Leinthall below a blot of a stone quarry. The larger village of Wigmore is situated to the half left where Roger Mortimer's ruined stronghold is situated (an English Heritage site open to the public free of charge).

Keep to the main grassy path as it cuts across the centre of the fort. Towards the other side, in front of the ramparts, stay on the main track as it loops to the right then swings left to descend around the base of the ramparts. You go over a stile and turn left on a crossing track and, after some fairly spectacular views to the right, shortly reach a junction of paths by a Forestry Commission sign. Keep the line more or less ahead along a grassy path on Mortimers Trail. Woodhampton and Sned Woods are visible now to your right and the village of Yatton is below.

After quite some distance, maybe about a third of a mile, you cross a stile and after a further 250 yards bear left at a fork to stay on Mortimers Trail. After a short distance turn right on reaching a junction with a forestry road. The views now become even better over the valley below towards Leintwardine and the Black Mountains in the distance. The track descends to reach a gateway and on the left, under the roof of a former building, is an information board about the area. ❷

Go through the gate and continue the descent on a tarmac lane. You pass to the left of a small black and white cottage and after a further 225 yards bear right by a timber waymark along Mortimers Trail again. There is an information board here also about Mortimers Cross and the battle of 1461 – see box on page 77. You cross a stile after about 80 yards and turn right to cross another after a further 100 yards or so. This is in fact a double stile and, after negotiating it, bear half left across a field to a waymarked fence stile in the tree line on the far boundary. Cross that and the next field directly heading for the tree line where

76

there is another fence stile to cross which takes you onto a narrow path descending into a wood.

The path winds down through attractive mixed woodland and you should take care – it can get slippery after wet weather. Eventually you go down a short flight of steps onto a broad crossing track – here depart from Mortimers Trail and turn left. After a while you can see the river Lugg down in the valley below. The path levels out and you walk parallel with the river for a time before moving away from it to go through a gate onto a grassy track between hedgerows. This track can get overgrown at times but soon opens out to continue along the bottom edge of a field. On arriving at a yard at the rear of a house go along the left side to emerge onto the B4362. Turn right here to walk the one third of a mile or so down to Mortimers Cross, the scene of a decisive battle in the Wars of the Roses. **❸**

Depending upon the time of your arrival, you may have time to take refreshment at the excellent Mortimers Cross pub before visiting the English Heritage Water Mill, if you wish to do so.

EH Mortimers Cross Water Mill

The mill is eighteenth century and was in commercial use for corn milling till the 1940s. It is still used occasionally to grind fodder for rare breeds animals on the adjacent farm. It is in private ownership but cared for by English Heritage and contains an exhibition relating to the battle. The actual site of the battle was on the meadows between the River Lugg and the A 4110, opposite the mill, and it took place on 2 February 1461. The Mortimers were central to the plot as Edmund Mortimer was the true heir to the throne having been named as his successor by the murdered Richard II. However, Edmund had died in 1425 and the claim passed to Richard Duke of York. The claim laid dormant until Henry VI proved unfit for Kingship and this was a signal for another Yorkist uprising. Richard was killed at Wakefield in 1460 by an army led by Henry's wife, Margaret of Anjou but his son, Edward, marched against the Queen and the two armies met at Mortimers Cross. The Lancastrians were outnumbered and, after a bloody battle, routed. Just under 4000 men were killed, about three-quarters of them Lancastrians, and many lie buried in the mound overlooking the battlefield.

Open on Thursdays, Sundays and BH Mondays 2pm-5pm April to September; entrance fee £2, £1.50 for children.
Tel. 01568 708820.

You should aim to leave Mortimers Cross by no later than 3pm and do so by crossing the stile directly opposite the Mill. Turn right and follow the field edge round alongside the River Lugg, on the opposite side of it to the battlesite. At the end of the field turn 90 degrees left along the adjacent side and then 90 degrees left again heading back up towards the road. After 100 yards go through a waymarked gate on your right – the second of two gates – into the next field. Follow the hedged boundary and, at the end, go through another waymarked gate and keep ahead in the next field.

You go through a further waymarked gate and continue the line forward on a rough track which passes to the right of a small pool. Go through yet another gate onto a track between hedgerows to exit via a gate onto a lane in the village of Lucton.

4

Turn right through the village (or if short of time turn left up to meet the main road again and skip to the start of the next paragraph) and follow the lane round the splendid Lucton Court. Shortly after that turn left at a junction along another lane towards the church. When you get there you will discover that the building is no longer a church but a superb residential conversion. On the bend opposite go over a stile into a meadow and walk along the right hedged boundary. The hedge loops right and as it straightens cross the strip of adjacent field to gain the tree line on your left and then follow that boundary round as it loops left. This sounds a little complicated but it isn't really. Look for a culvert bridge over the brook on your left which takes you into a field on the other side and cross that field diagonally to the top left corner where there is a fence stile and steps down to the main road.

Cross directly onto a narrow lane going uphill (no through road) for about a quarter of a mile passing a cottage on the right then another a little further on just before what appears to be the remains of an old bridge. Here take the waymarked path on the right immediately after the second cottage. You go under an arbour of laurel into a wooded area which becomes denser as you go along. If walking in May the rhododendrons here are spectacular. You soon meet a junction with a broader track and turn right onto it through very pleasant mixed woodland, again with lots of rhododendrons. As the track veers left continue ahead for a few yards to cross a large fence stile into a field. The ground may be boggy on the other side as a stream runs down the edge of the field!

From here set out across the field on more or less the same line towards a fence which you should be able to see on the far boundary in the tree line about 300 yards away. The town of Leominster is visible over to your right from here. There may be some boggy bits in the field to skirt around but, on arrival at the fence, I hope you will find a National Trust notice about the avenue of Spanish Chestnuts beyond. *The trees are suffering from a fungal disease called 'ink disease' and it has become necessary to exclude the public and stock. The triple avenue is the only one of its kind in the country and the Trust are investigating ways of saving it from further damage.*

The right of way has been diverted at this point and you should turn left in front of the fence along the field edge for 30 yards and cross a stile in the corner. Cross another stile immediately on the right into the adjacent field and walk along the bottom edge of it alongside the chestnut avenue. At the end bear round to the left for a few yards before crossing a fence on your right or the awkward little stile to the side of it.

You are now in a pasture field and continue alongside the fenced off avenue. The effects of the disease are clear to see. Over to the left now is a double avenue of lime trees. At the end of the chestnut avenue turn left to pass under the limes and continue ahead to join a fence line in front of you, at which point turn right to walk with it on your left. You will now see Croft Castle to the half right and at the end of the field go through a gate onto a broad track. You pass Garden Cottage and go through another gate and across the top of the farmyard. You go through yet another gate and keep ahead on a tarmac surface around the rear of outbuildings to return to the starting point. With a bit of luck there should be time enough for a change of footwear and a look round the Castle.

14

Ancient Churches of Herefordshire

Maps: Landranger 149, 150; Pathfinder 973, 995; Explorer 202.
Start: From Edvin Loach Old Church about 4½ miles north of Bromyard off the B4203. Some 2½ miles after leaving the town, take the first turning left and follow the lane until reaching the Church – it is signed. Those travelling from the north will turn right in Tedstone Wafer and follow the road round to same point. GR 663584.
Distance: The whole walk is a long one – some 13½ miles – so to attempt it you need staying power and allow plenty of time. It is also a little more adventurous than many in the book with the possibility of ploughed fields etc. and careful attention to route finding is required in parts so, if these things bother you, give it a miss. You can, if you wish, divide the walk into two parts of roughly equal distance and make a return visit – see text.
Terrain: A pleasant ramble through the scenic Herefordshire countryside with stops along the way to visit some of the area's historic churches. A few short climbs but nothing too strenuous. Some fields may be planted in the summer months and I would say that the best times to do this walk are Spring and Autumn.
Refreshments: One public house en route, The Gate Hangs Well at Lower Sapey.

Edvin Loach Church

THE name Edvin Loach is derived from the de Loges family who owned land here in the late eleventh century. The old church may have been built during this time by Saxons under Norman direction. Unfortunately, after the new church was built in the 1860s it was allowed to fall into ruin although there is still a fine example of herringbone masonry, typical of Norman churches in the area. It is now in the safekeeping of English Heritage. Access available free at any reasonable time. The 'new' Church of St. Mary is stunningly beautiful with an unusual semi-circular Chancel. If you go inside read the wall plaque about Edwyn Ralph, the next church on the route.

From the church retreat to the lane and turn right. On the way down you may, on a clear day, be able to pick out Titterstone Clee to your left and the Malverns to the right. After a little under a quarter of a mile you reach a large farm and,

80

opposite the farmhouse, branch off right up a broad waymarked track. Ignore a stile on the left as the track curves right but then take the second of two left turnings immediately following, which brings you into a field. Follow the left boundary and after a while the ground dips towards a cottage at the bottom of the field. You skirt around the right side of the cottage (diversion from definitive route) and go over a fence stile on your left to continue ahead in the adjacent field to the left of a post and wire fence.

At the end of this field follow the bottom boundary around for 20 yards and go through a gate on your right onto a narrow path through undergrowth and out into a plantation of small trees which slopes downwards. You need to pick the best way you can through the trees but keep on the downward course and at some point you will spot a residence ahead. Aim for that and in the bottom boundary there is a footbridge. Cross this then a paddock diagonally to the top left corner. Here go over two waymarked stiles onto a tarmac driveway by the residence (Bodkin Hall) and turn right in a direction away from it.

Continue on the driveway until you reach a waymarked junction with another driveway and turn right. The way loops round to go through a gate and you now stay on this course to

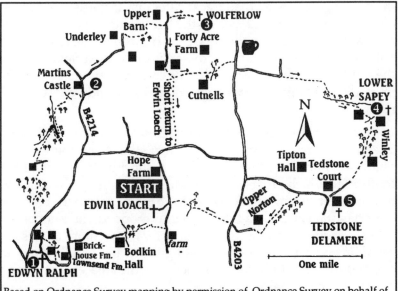

Based on Ordnance Survey mapping by permission of Ordnance Survey on behalf of the Controller of Her Majesty's Stationery Office, © Crown Copyright MC 100005051.

Edwyn Ralph Church

pass, firstly, Brickhouse Farm then Townsend Farm (ignoring all waymarks into adjacent fields) to arrive at Edwyn Ralph Church.

❶

On leaving the church turn left to continue along the lane but only for about 50 yards before you veer right at a waymark through a gate onto a broad track. After just 15 yards you need to cross a stile in a timber fence on the left to enter a field and, once over and facing farm buildings, bear right to a stile close to the bottom right corner. Having crossed into the next field, keep to the right hedged boundary and at the end cross another stile to be immediately confronted with yet another stile and a gate on your right.

Do not cross this stile but bear left into a narrow field and, after a few yards, go right over a further stile. After doing so you will find yourself in a small thicket. A short distance ahead is a footbridge which brings you out into a facing field in which you bear half left cutting off the corner to go over a stile in the crossing boundary 80 yards ahead. If the field is cropped you may prefer to walk around the edge. Continue forward on more or less the same line over the next field passing to the left of a lone oak to another stile about 150 yards further on in the adjacent boundary. Again this field could be cropped.

Cross the stile onto a metalled farm track and go directly over this following the waymark into a pasture field. Bear right here alongside a mixed tree boundary and continue round to reach a stile which you cross into a narrow field – go diagonally left over this to a stile in the opposite boundary roughly midway between two gates. This takes you onto a narrow path between beech trees which shortly emerges onto a tarmac driveway. You go over that and continue on a narrow path to cross a stile into a field. Bear half left in the field around to the rear of a bungalow to gain and cross a further stile in the hedge bordering the B4214.

Turn left on the road for about 30 yards before crossing to follow a waymarked path alongside new houses. This continues as it borders a pasture field and emerges onto a track which you cross directly onto a narrow path between trees and fence. The path twists around some more properties and to the right of a paddock before coming to a stile. Cross this and the end of the paddock diagonally towards the bottom left corner, close to which you will find another waymarked stile leading you into a wood.

After a short distance you go over a small footbridge into a field and turn right to walk along the bottom edge of it. Stay with the boundary as it turns left on a rising course (there is a permissive diversion here from the O.S.plan which shows the path cutting left across the field but it seems the intention is that you continue with the boundary) as it kinks right then left to reach the top of the field. This is a much more sensible alternative to crossing it when it is ploughed up! As you reach the top of the incline magnificent views open up ahead over Titterstone Clee.

You emerge from the field onto a metalled driveway to a farmhouse which you have been able to see for a while over to your left. Some attention is required to direction along this next section and you should read the remainder of this paragraph before proceeding. Turn right onto the driveway then immediately left through a gate into a sloping pasture field. The correct route now stays parallel with the left boundary alongside the farm driveway to reach a stone outbuilding opposite the farmhouse then, from the waymarked gate just beyond, strikes 90 degrees right down the field passing to the right of an oak tree 120 yards away (not the tree further to your left) and onwards to meet a fence line and trees coming in from the right. This is not difficult if the field is in pasture but, if it is ploughed or planted, you may wish to consider turning right through the gate into the field and walking around the boundary to follow it down to the said fence line. Whichever, when you get there, you start to divert away from the trees to the very bottom left corner of the field to go through a gate.

At the end of the next field bear right along the adjacent boundary down a sunken track to another gate and, once through, bear left on a narrow track which loops right onto a causeway across a lake. Once on the other side go up an embankment to a waymarked gate. DO NOT GO THROUGH but keep left on a track still within the wooded area with the lake now on your left. Where the path goes left to follow the lake continue straight ahead to descend a short bank and through a small gate into a meadow. Now go forward to the right of a wood and stream climbing gently until you pass through a sparse hedge line. At this point bear right, away from the stream, to reach a metal gate in the top boundary of the field to the left of an open copse and under an oak tree.

Go through the gate and follow a bridle path along the right of a hedge line and through another gate before continuing ahead across the next field to a further gate clearly visible in the opposite tree line. Go through and cross the subsequent culvert then follow a sunken track directly ahead as it curves upwards and to the right to meet a hedged boundary. Continue with this boundary on your left towards Martin's Castle Farm and at the end of the field go through a waymarked gate onto the farm drive. Turn right here and in 100 yards join the B4214 where you turn left. ❷

Cross the road, ignore the right turn to Ripplewood, and after 250 yards or so turn off right down a waymarked metalled driveway. As you walk along the impressive Georgian farmhouse of Underley imposes itself on your left and you bear left in front of some cottages before reaching the property. The driveway takes you to the right of the house, through a gate and then another adjacent to the farmyard after which branch off immediately right up a shale track. Almost immediately again take the second gate on your right, which is waymarked, into a pasture field.

Keep to the right edge of the field on a rising course where views open up to the left over Titterstone Clee and the South Shropshire countryside. The climb over roughish ground is fairly punishing on the leg muscles but at the end loop left along the top of the field and around the base of a small hill, through a waymarked gate into a field where you continue the climb along the right boundary. After only about 50 yards, however, the ground begins to level out and you go through a timber gate on your right followed by a metal one into a field where you walk to the right of a tall hawthorn hedge.

You are led out onto a concrete driveway and turn left onto it. Shortly Wolferlow Church comes into view over to the right and after about 120 yards, opposite Upper Barn, take the waymarked path over a fence stile on your right into a young plantation. Stay with the left boundary and cross another fence stile to stay on the same course from where you can see the splendid black and white elevations of Wolferlow Court ahead. Go through a gate in the field boundary on your left just before reaching the church which takes you onto a tarmac driveway then on a short distance to the church itself. ❸

On leaving retreat back over the field/paddock to exit onto the concrete driveway again and now turn left onto it. You pass the point of your earlier exit onto the driveway and continue on it, ignoring a waymark to the right after another quarter of a mile, until reaching a farm. A waymark on a fence post as you approach the farm directs you forward between the farmhouse and barns to a gate in front of a large field. Once through the gate cut half left in a large field to a point (which you cannot immediately see) about 50 yards to the left of where a hedge line

St. Andrews Church, Wolferlow

ST. ANDREWS is stone built church with a timber spire hung with shingles, which is typical of this area. The upper part is nineteenth century although the timbers are medieval and there are some Norman remains. There is an unidentified thirteenth century stone carved effigy of a lady dressed in a wimple (worn by nuns) and, at her feet, an animal which may be a dog but looks more like a lion. (acknowledgement, D.M.Annett, *An Informal Guide to the Churches of the Bromyard Rural Deanery, 1987*)

Inside are warnings about the poor structural condition and defective roof caused by 'inappropriate repairs'. You can see the lathe and plaster coming off the walls and a net has been provided to catch the crumbling material. A very sad state of affairs unfortunately so please take care when looking around.

begins on the far side. Please ignore the stile at the right end of the hedge line. At the point described you will find a footbridge hidden behind a jutting-in corner of an adjacent field.

You can now return to Edvin Loach from here and the directions for this follow. If planning to complete the entire walk please skip to the beginning of the next but one paragraph. Cross the footbridge and turn left across the field to the top left corner but, if this is difficult because of crops, you may wish to consider walking around the edge to the same point where there is another footbridge to cross then a waymarked stile leading you into the next field. The correct route is straight ahead on a course about 50 yards to the left of the boundary passing to the right of a lone oak, where there is a waymark post, to arrive at a fence stile in a crossing boundary. Again a route along the edge might seem preferable if the field is planted.

Cross the stile and continue directly ahead in the ensuing field to a gate in another crossing boundary 150 yards ahead. There is another fence stile to cross adjacent to the gate and in the next field you stay close to the left boundary hedge and,at the end, there are two gates. Take the one directly ahead as waymarked into a long field and follow the left boundary to the end where you emerge onto a lane via a gate. Turn right on the lane then left at a junction after 250 yards and stay on this lane past Hope Farm to return to Edvin Loach after a further third of a mile or so.

If attempting the full walk, DO NOT CROSS THE FOOTBRIDGE, even though the waymark invites you to. Instead turn left in front of it down the same field with the boundary on your right to reach a stile and footbridge at the bottom which you cross into an open field. The way is directly across the field aiming for the left end of a tall hedge line on the opposite boundary – Forty Acre Farm is over to the left and 'Cutnells' on the right. This field may well be planted and, if passage is difficult, you may have to consider turning left to walk around the edge. Just to the left of the hedge referred to is a just about passable gap into the next field where you follow the hedged boundary.

At the bottom of the field continue through a gap in the boundary through a scrubby area of ground to the left of a fence and down an embankment to cross a footbridge. Once over follow the waymark to the right through some trees to emerge into a field where you bear left to follow the edge with a tree line on your left then, at the corner turn right along the adjacent boundary. The correct route on emergence into the field is to go half left across it but this is one of those paths which boundary changes have made illogical and I can see no good reason for following it strictly. You can, of course, do so if you wish and in this case you should aim for an ash tree on the left boundary and turn right. Whichever route you take continue upwards along the long field edge towards buildings in view and exit through a gap onto a lane. If ready for a break turn left here and The Gate Hangs Well will shortly be reached on your right.

On leaving retrace your steps past your exit point onto the lane (or turn right here if not visiting the pub) and after 100 yards turn off left down a lane signed Harpley. You walk along this pleasant lane for a little while, with good views of the Malverns over to the right, until it swings sharp left. Here you turn right onto a broad stone farm track and continue on it through one gate, then the right-hand of a pair of gates onto a green lane and past a derelict farmhouse. Follow the green lane until it opens out into a field and you stay on the same line across it before going through a gate on the far boundary after about 120 yards and out into an open field. Now bear very slightly to the left to a gate which you can see on the opposite side. Go through and turn right to follow the boundary down looping left around a small wood then keeping to the tree line as it swings right to the bottom

St. Bartholomew's Old Church

THIS beautiful old church is situated in the most enchanting place on a country lane which appears to go nowhere. It has a real atmosphere and although no longer used for services it remains consecrated and is in the care of the Churches Conservation Trust.

St. Bartholomew's dates from the end of the eleventh century with most of the present structure originating from the twelfth century. The three small Norman windows survive and the south doorway is also Norman. The pine gallery was added at the beginning of the nineteenth century, as were the box pews and pulpit. This is an important building historically and architecturally and there are leaflets available with much more information for those who are interested.

of the field. Continue ahead here into the wood where you cross over a stream and shortly bear left onto a broad track. Stay on this for a while until going through a gate by a black and white farmhouse to arrive at St. Bartholomew's Old Church, Lower Sapey. ❹

I have a small confession here and, if I don't make it, someone is sure to take me to task. The boundary between Herefordshire and Worcestershire weaves around this area and you have in fact now crossed over the border into Worcestershire. St. Bartholomew's is really an ancient church of Worcestershire but I hope you will forgive this little bit of poetic licence. Before you reach the last stop off point at Tedstone Delamere you cross the border again into Herefordshire.

Now go up the shale track opposite towards a large house and pass round to the left of it and turn left to follow the garden hedge to a gate in a post & wire fence. Go through this into the adjacent field and keep to the left boundary. At the end of the field go through a gap on the left then turn immediately right through a gate to continue along a track following the same line as before. This track descends through an area of young trees then swings right to go through another gate (which has a stream running at the back of it so the ground can get muddy!) then up an embankment, after which keep tight on the right boundary over undulating ground to enter a broad track heading towards Winley Farm.

You go though another gate to arrive at a junction with the farm driveway and you cross this directly to the right of a barn, go through a further gate and emerge into an orchard. Continue the line across the orchard to the far left corner and go through a gate and bear half left across another orchard to a fence stile in front of a wood after a further 120 yards or so. Cross then take care down an embankment onto what could be an overgrown path into the trees. You go over a footbridge and continue to the top of an incline where there is a broader track which you turn right onto.

Again this track can get overgrown in summer but should be passable. You emerge at a junction with a farm track and turn right to arrive immediately at a junction with another track where you continue ahead uphill passing to the right of the farm. The track turns to tarmac and goes by some cottages, climbing

Tedstone Delemere Church

steadily before straightening and taking you to the rear of the palatial looking Tedstone Court and a junction with a lane in the settlement of Tedstone Delamere. Turn left past the entrance to 'Gracefields' with its attractive converted oasthouses, then turn left again after 50 yards or so, just after the front entrance to Tedstone Court, through a kissing gate to visit the church. ❺

Return to the lane and retrace your steps past your earlier entrance point onto it and continue on the lane as it starts to rise.

Church of St. James, Tedstone Delamere

A PLAQUE on the small car park on the lane states this to be an eleventh century foundation although little remains from that period. The Church of St. James is, however, of considerable age and was restored in the mid nineteenth century. The remaining Norman parts are built from a local stone called 'tufa' which has a sponge-like appearance and there is some interesting stained glass, that in the east window by the celebrated nineteenth century maker, John Hardman, who made some of the wonderful glass in Worcester Cathedral. By the lychgate is an eighteenth century 'chest tomb' topped by an urn and backed by dark yew – the whole thing now rather faded. The church is now administered by Herefordshire Historic Churches Trust. (Acknowledgement, D.M Annett, *An Informal Guide to the Churches of the Bromyard Rural Deanery, 1987.*)

89

Shortly after passing the right turn to Tipton Hall you reach the top of the incline and look for a waymarked stile on your left which takes you into a field. Cross another, rather awkward, stile after 40 yards in the tree line on your right then turn left to continue the same line forward but now with the tree line on your left. Look carefully again now for a post on your left with yellow marker tape after only about 25 yards and a small stile at the bottom of a short embankment – very easily missed if you are not concentrating! Go through the gate into an avenue of trees bordering the field (NOT along the field edge itself). There is yellow marker tape at intervals to guide you but the way is not difficult to follow although it may be nettly in summer.

At the end cross a stile into a field and stay on line with a tree line on your left. Go through a gate into the next field still on the same line, through another gate in a crossing boundary, ignoring a hunters stile on the left, and continue ahead through the next crossing boundary of hawthorn trees, after which you can see Upper Norton House in view. The next field undulates but stay close to the left boundary past a large oak with a tree house in it to reach a waymarked stile close to the top left corner. This takes you down a fairly steep embankment to another stile with a choice of routes. Go right towards the farm, climbing the lawn to walk directly in front of the farmhouse, where there is a good view backwards over Herefordshire countryside to the east of Bromyard including the palatial Whitbourne Hall, now converted to flats. Most people will feel uncomfortable walking through a private garden and I believe here that the owners are seeking approval to establish a permissive route taking walkers away from the house. It may perhaps be that this has been done by the time this book is published. If not, go forward and bear right though a gravelled courtyard and exit between stone pillars to reach a junction with a tarmac driveway. Turn left onto the driveway and follow it until it exits onto the B4023.

Cross the road directly through a waymarked gate keeping to the right of a field boundary. You cross a footbridge followed by a stile to emerge into open pasture where a waymark directs you slightly right towards the top right corner. Before the corner in the hedge on your right is a stile which you cross to stay on the same line over another field heading towards the left end of a tree line on the opposite side. In the field is planted you may wish to consider turning left to walk around the edge.

The ground dips to a stile, which is awkward to cross with steps down the other side. Once over stay on line through the next field down towards a tree line below where there is another stile and footbridge. Take care as the ground between them can get boggy. This brings you into yet another pasture field where you continue directly forward to the opposite boundary where the corner of an adjacent field juts in, then turn left in front of it to walk uphill with the boundary on your right. At the top cross a stile onto a narrow lane then go forward along a metalled track signed Edvin Loach Church to return to the starting point.

15

Arthur's Stone

Maps: Outdoor Leisure 13.
Start: At Arthur's Stone in Arthur's Stone Lane, two miles south-west of the village of Bredwardine which is located on the B4352 between Hereford and Hay-on-Wye. From the direction of the latter, proceed through Bredwardine and take a right turn after half a mile (or turn sharp left before the village if approaching from the Hereford direction) then turn right again after another mile following the brown signs. Parking spaces at the Stone are limited and I would suggest using the grass verges nearby in order to leave the spaces available for short stay visitors. GR 318432.
Distance: 6 miles.
Terrain: Undulating countryside with superb views across this section of the Wye Valley and to the south towards The Black Mountains. There is a sharp descent into Bredwardine and, I'm afraid, a steep ascent near the end. Please do not attempt unless reasonably fit.
Refreshments: The Red Lion Hotel at Bredwardine. Meals and snacks served.

Arthur's Stone

ARTHUR'S STONE is an impressive multi-chambered tomb of the Neolithic period or New Stone Age, between 3700 and 2700BC. These people lived in small communities of 25-100 and tombs such as this were used to bury their dead over several generations. Raising of the great roof stone, which is now patially collapsed, was a considerable feat with only simple tools. The name of Arthur's Stone is derived from folklore which would have us believe that the Stone marks the site of one of King Arthur's battles even though the legend dates from thousands of years after the tomb was built!

Access is free at any reasonable time.

WITH your back to the Stone turn left, ignoring a footpath opposite, and walk along the lane for about 200 yards before branching off right through a gate into a field on a waymarked bridleway. At the end of the field cross a fence stile and keep the same line over the next field heading towards the

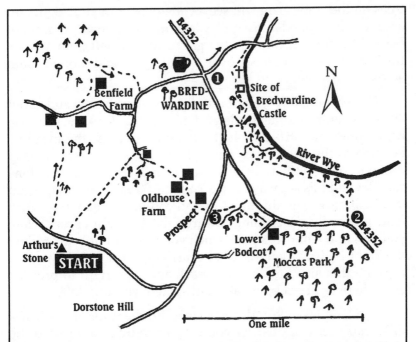

Based on Ordnance Survey mapping by permission of Ordnance Survey on behalf of the Controller of Her Majesty's Stationery Office, © Crown Copyright MC 100005051.

left edge of a group of conifers, effectively slicing off the left side of the field. You will arrive at the field corner and cross a fence stile into a downward sloping field, ignoring a gate on the left. There are good views now to the north and west with Dinmore Hill over to the right.

Follow the left boundary of the field and, at the end, cross a stile then bear half left diagonally down the next field to the left of a belt of trees ahead. When you get there continue downwards parallel with the right boundary fence over undulating ground towards a cottage in the valley below. On the way you will pass by what is described on the O.S. plan as a 'disused pit' and at the bottom cross a stile on the right to gain a grassy track which leads across the front of the cottage to reach a junction with a lane.

Turn right on the lane but after only 120 yards, opposite Oak Cottage, take the waymarked bridleway on your left through a gate into an upward sloping pasture field. Take a little care of direction now. Follow the waymark indicator half right, keeping to the lower section of the field and passing to the right of a line of trees on the slope. You will see a cottage over to your right and are then channelled into a gulley leading to a gateway in front of Benfield farm. Go through the gate and bear left onto a stone track past the farmhouse, over a cattle grid and along a path across a meadow.

On reaching a waymark post by a telegraph pole and about 80 yards before another cattle grid, turn to face back the way you have come and strike off half left up and across the meadow keeping to the left of two trees. At the top of the first rise drop down to pass to the right of an oak then aim directly for a lone ash. Beyond this is a waymark post some 80 yards ahead in a gap in a hedgerow – go through this and continue ahead in the next field gradually descending towards the far right corner. Here you will find a hunter's gate which you pass through and follow the right hedged boundary until arriving at a metal gate. Go through this also onto a stony track and turn right to proceed along here until emerging at a lane, where you turn left.

The lane takes you down a steep gradient for about half a mile into Bredwardine. As you may have by now realised the converse of that well known law 'what goes up must come down' will apply at some stage on the walk in order to re-gain the start. Unfortunately, as I said in the introductory notes, this will come close to the end so I will apologise in advance for that! The Red Lion Hotel is located at the village crossroads if you wish to take refreshment. **❶**

The Red Lion is a seventeenth century free house and externally, at the front at least, it has not altered a great deal. Until quite recently the local magistrates met there in the 'Court Room'. The name Bredwardine means 'place on the slope of a steep ridge' and, as you will have just learned, the name is an apt one. It has a famous son in the Rev. Francis Kilvert whose diary of Victorian life achieved world-wide acclaim. It was published in three volumes in 1938-40 and became the subject of a BBC television series. Sadly, Kilvert died in 1879 of peritonitis at the age of 38 and five weeks after his marriage. He is buried in the churchyard of Bredwardine Church, which you will have the opportunity of visiting shortly. Now a Kilvert Society keeps alive interest in his work.

Go over the crossroads towards the river Wye for about a third of a mile, noting on the left a fourteenth century stone building known as 'Old Court'. Just before the bridge crossing take the waymarked path down to your right into a meadow bordering the river. If you look back at the bridge you will see that it is quite some structure. Six arched and 30 feet above river level it was built in 1762-4 as a toll bridge, charging ½d per foot traveller, 1d for a horse or 3d if the horse was drawing a cart and 10d per score of cattle. You quickly cross a footbridge then depart from the river up the pasture field towards Bredwardine Church. Cross a stile in front of the church and follow the track off to the right to visit it. The building is basically Norman with a Georgian tower and has some interesting features. At the north end are two effigies – one a man of great stature, reputedly Walter Baskerville, Lord of the Manor, who died in 1369 and the other a knight, believed to be Sir Roger Vaughan who was killed at the Battle of Agincourt in 1415 defending Henry V.

Continue on the path around to the rear of the church, go through a waymarked gate into a meadow and bear right onto a sunken path which takes you to the left of an apple orchard, one of the many which grow fruit to make the cider for which Herefordshire is justly famous. The path goes under an arbour of mixed trees to arrive at a junction. Here turn right and almost immediately go over a crossing track – do not enter the path (or any of the paths) on your left into the thicker area of trees. Over to your left is a tree covered mound which was once the site of Bredwardine Castle, one of a chain built to protect the Welsh border, and nearer on your left a sunken area of ground which were fish ponds serving the castle.

After a while the path curves right to go through a waymarked gate before passing to the right of a small private lake. Go over a footbridge at the far end of the lake, after which ignore a stile on your right. You join and turn right at a broader track shortly before reaching another stile by a stream. The stile is totally superfluous as there is a large gap to the side of it and you still have to cross the stream. Bear right after crossing on a grassy track and through a gate after traversing a small rise, then bear left with the waymark and off the broad track out into a field. Follow the left boundary fence now ignoring all paths left into the wood (however tempting they may be!)

At the end of a long field you will go through another waymarked gate to continue on a broad grassy track. You may catch occasional glimpses of the river as you walk along, although in high summer these are likely to be blotted out by trees in leaf. Cross a stile into a pasture field which slopes down to the river and stay with the top post & wire boundary until, at the end, you cross a waymarked stile on the right into the adjacent field. Follow the left boundary hedge going away from the river to gain a road and turn right. **❷**

You need to walk along this road for about a third of a mile and there is no footpath, so please take care. Moccas Deer Park is over to your left and you pass an isolated cottage before turning off left after a further 120 yards up a narrow lane. After a short climb you arrive at some apparently derelict farm buildings with an attractive farmhouse at the rear (Lower Bodcot). Directly opposite the derelict buildings turn right through a metal gate into what might be a boggy paddock. There are now three gates facing you on the opposite side and a waymark directs you through the gate to the right into a pasture field where you strike out ahead towards a waymark post in the middle of the field.

At the end of the field you cross a culverted stream and stile to turn left and cross a further stile 50 yards ahead by a brook. Now bear half right diagonally across an undulating pasture field cutting off the right corner of it to a stile on an embankment after 120 yards in a crossing boundary. Cross the stile and the next field on the same line to another stile and waymark 120 yards further on which exits onto a lane. **❸**

Cross the lane directly onto a tarmacked bridleway which soon turns stony. You pass a farmhouse called 'Prospect' then arrive at Oldhouse Farm, where you need to be careful to take the right route. You pass to the right of the farmhouse and go through a waymarked gate. Almost immediately there is another gate but do not go through it – instead turn left in front of the second gate, between the farm buildings and out into a sloping field following the bottom post & wire boundary. When you reach an open gateway after 100 yards into an adjacent field don't go through but divert left to continue ahead in the same field but now with a hedge as the right boundary. In fact you should strictly be walking at a distance of about 30 yards from it to meet a waymarked timber gate in the top boundary.

Go through this gate (ignoring the gate in the corner on your right and the one immediately to the left) and in the next field follow the right boundary hedge in a line parallel but some way off a wood over to your left. At the end there is another

Arthur's Stone

waymarked gate which leads onto a broad track between hedgerows with a stream running along it. Just before coming to a junction and opposite a stone cottage look carefully for a fence stile on your left and cross it into an upward sloping field. The best way now is to scramble up the embankment on the right to gain even ground and follow the left boundary as it rises to a fence stile at the end.

Here is the hard bit! Once over continue a steep ascent to the right of some trees but, as you pause for breath, take a look backwards at the expansive views over the Wye Valley towards Hereford and beyond. After an energy sapping climb you are obliged to cross an awkward fence stile and the next short field directly before negotiating a further stile into a large open pasture. Bear just slightly right over this field to find the next stile in a small tree line in the far boundary and, once over that, continue the line forward gradually closing with the top left corner of a further field with a farm over to the left. Here cross a stile and proceed to the top corner of the ensuing field to cross yet another stile before continuing to the right of a hedged boundary. At the end cross the final stile onto the lane in front of Arthur's Stone.

16

Goodrich Castle and Symonds Yat

Maps: Outdoor Leisure (yellow cover) 14.
Start: The car park to Goodrich Castle. From the A40 about four miles south of Ross-on-Wye there is a well signed turning to Goodrich, which is only a short distance from the main road. GR577197.
Distance: 6 miles or 10 miles.
Terrain: Pleasant easy walking along the banks of the River Wye followed by a strenuous climb up to Symonds Yat Rock, rewarded by stunning views over the Wye Valley.
Refreshments: There is a refreshments kiosk at the Castle and a café at Symonds Yat. Also a public house in Goodrich.

! It's your choice whether to visit the Castle before or after the walk but, if you intend to do the whole ten mile circuit, give some thought to time available. Although the Castle has quite long opening hours (see below) you do not want to leave insufficient time to visit it or, conversely, find yourself having to rush the walk.

EH   Goodrich Castle

GOODRICH CASTLE is a magnificent red sandstone stronghold and remarkably well preserved. It dates mainly from the thirteenth and fourteenth centuries, although the keep is twelfth century, and was built here to overlook and command an important ford across the River Wye. In particular, its position on a spur of rock above the ford prevented the Welsh using the crossing as a route to attack England in the thirteenth century. It was subjected to a long siege by Parliamentary forces in the Civil War, after which it was rendered uninhabitable. There is a maze of rooms and passageways to explore and some wonderful views.

Open: 1 April to 30 Sept, 10 am to 6 pm; 1 to 31 Oct, 10 am to 5 pm; 1 Nov to 31 Mar, 10am to 1pm, 2pm to 4pm. Closed 24-26 Dec, 1 Jan.
Admission: £3.20/ £2.40/ £1.60.Inclusive of audio tour.
Tel: 01600 890538.

WALK away from the Castle down the lane to a junction. Proceed ahead for a few yards to another junction with the lane running through Cruse village and turn left (do not turn left at the first junction referred to along a more minor lane). You go past a school on your right and after about 125 yards you arrive at another junction, this time with a more major road and here turn left again. Please take care as it is fairly busy and there is not a footpath. You shortly go under a road bridge after which there is a narrow path on the right to walk along.

You pass on the left what used to be Flanesford Priory, now converted into holiday accommodation. Flanesford was founded by Richard Talbot after his return from the battle of Crecy in 1349 and the surviving building was probably the monks dining hall. On arrival at a bridge over the River Wye, turn right just before it following the waymark for the Wye Valley Walk down some steps and onto a path in a field bordering the river.

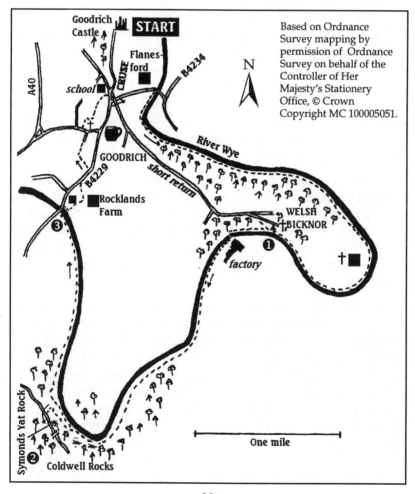

Based on Ordnance Survey mapping by permission of Ordnance Survey on behalf of the Controller of Her Majesty's Stationery Office, © Crown Copyright MC 100005051.

As the path and the river curve left you cross a waymarked stile then another shortly afterwards before climbing some steps into a wood to continue on an elevated path above the river. Ignore a waymark right to Goodrich and further on cross a stile where the trees open out a little into a narrow field. There is a chalet site on the opposite side of the river. After a while you go over another stile in a crossing fence and continue ahead alongside the river on a broad grassy path. You shortly cross a further stile and pass the rather attractive looking Courtfield Arms – on the other side of the river unfortunately! Courtfield itself (or what was Courtfield but now called The Mill Fathers) is the group of properties on the top of the hill to your right and is a religious retreat.

On approaching the hamlet of Welsh Bicknor you cross a stile, then another before arriving at an interesting looking church with a Celtic cross in the churchyard. Regrettably it is kept locked which, to our great loss, are so many churches these days. After the church you pass in front of a Youth Hostel and ascend a concrete ramp, at the top of which is an information board about the Wye Valley Walk stretching for a distance of 75 miles between Chepstow and Hay-on-Wye. At the top of the ramp continue ahead still parallel with the river but a little further away from it. **❶**

There is a waymark on the right back to the castle which can be taken by those wishing to shorten the walk. It leads you onto a steeply rising path through woods before coming out to join the driveway to the Youth Hostel. Continue forward on an uphill track which has now turned to tarmac, turn left at a junction then follow the lane all the way back to the castle – a distance of about two miles.

If intent upon completing the distance continue past the waymark and cross the river via a bridge leading to a large blot of a factory. If you look to your right before doing so you will see a tunnel hewn out of the rock and will note that the bridge itself is a former rail crossing. Turn left now down some steps and go under the bridge to pick up the river path but on the other side to that walked up to this point. You shortly cross a stile by a quaint fishing lodge (Lydbrook Fishery) and then proceed along field edges to cross two more – note the line of the old railway marked by the fence line over to your left – before ascending a flight of steps into a wooded area. You soon exit the wood by a complicated stile and now actually join the old line in the form of a broad grassy path and follow it for some time, with the river below.

After a while you enter onto an attractive section of river with the spectacular Coldwell Rocks in view ahead. Continue across a fence stile and then a normal stile by a gate before reaching a waymark post on your left just in front of an elevated residence. Now this is where you need to shake off that false sense of security created by a nice leisurely stroll along the river bank! You do not have to venture upwards (you can simply carry on the main path and skip the next two paragraphs) but, if choosing to do so, I can promise that the effort will be more than rewarded by some marvellous views.

Divert left at the waymark on a narrow path to the rear of the house which then winds through the trees on a course which is in fact fairly gradual although it does become more steep around the remote cottage of Wren's Nest. Towards the top of the incline there is a path going off to your right and which would be your return route except that it was closed at the time of research for repair. On eventually reaching a lane turn left to maintain the upward momentum for about 250 yards before turning right up a path which leads you over a bridge across the lane and onto Yat

Coldwell Rocks and the River Wye

101

Rock. From here there are superb views over the river valley and also an RSPB observation point concentrating on Peregrine Falcons which, at the time of my visit, were nesting on Coldwell Rocks. **❷**

When ready to resume retrace your steps and, if the path referred to above is open, turn left along it and descend to meet a broad shale track. Cross it directly to follow a waymark down some uneven steps onto a narrow path between trees. If the path is still closed you have no choice but to retrace all the way down to the start of the climb and turn left, passing beneath the elevated house and by another old tunnel. Join and continue ahead along a broad shale track which starts to rise. Part the way up the incline turn off right at a waymark down some uneven steps onto a narrow path between trees. You pass by a derelict cottage and come out again by the river, where the path can get overgrown in summer.

You shortly come upon a tiny cottage with a manicured lawn and rock garden in a most beautiful spot. After the cottage go up some steps and at a fork in the path keep to the lower path parallel with the river. You soon leave the trees behind and continue on the path along the top of the river bank. At the end of a long field go through a crossing boundary into another field and, at the end of this, cross a footbridge into the next field. The end of this one brings you to a road where you turn right to cross a bridge over the river. There is a narrow footpath only so care is required. **❸**

Immediately after the bridge take the waymarked path right to Ferry Cottage. You pass right in front of the cottage and through a small gate into a field where you bear left. You are now heading towards Rockwell Farm and cross a stile to continue ahead over a driveway to the gothic looking house towards the farmyard. Do not enter the farmyard, however, but take the path to the left alongside a stone wall to cross a stile then almost immediately go through a gate to continue ahead to the left of the farm buildings. You quickly go through two more gates before turning left at a junction on a track exiting onto the B4229 via a stile.

Turn right along the road – please take care as there is no footpath – and after a distance of about 200 yards cross the road and turn off left at a waymark through a wicket gate into a field.

Follow the direction indicated half right across the field and as you gradually climb you will see a stile in the left corner and another one ahead. Go for the latter, cross and then take a bearing half left, although effectively continuing the line forward from the previous field, aiming for the top right corner about 125 yards away. Here there is another stile to cross onto a grassy path which quickly turns to stone and passes between dwellings to reach a junction with a tarmac lane.

Turn left on the lane and after 40 yards bear right following a waymark between houses towards St. Giles Church. Again the church is unfortunately kept locked although there are details of the key holder posted if you would like to look inside. Pass to the right of the church and take the left path at a fork by its entrance and exit through a kissing gate at the rear. This leads out onto a narrow path along the edge of a field and you go through another kissing gate onto a path down a sloping field to a gateway in a line of poplar trees. Go through and cross the school field to a gate on the opposite side which exits onto a lane. Turn left then right to retrace steps back to the castle car park.

Goodrich Castle

Worcestershire

17

Harvington Hall

> **Maps:** Landranger 139; Pathfinder 953; Explorer 219.
> **Start:** At Harvington Hall which is located just off the A450 about three miles east of Kidderminster centre. Take the A448 Bromsgrove Road out of the town and, on reaching Mustow Green, bear left to Harvington. GR 878745.
> **Distance:** 6½ miles.
> **Terrain:** Fairly easy going over gently undulating countryside. No climbs of any note.
> **Refreshments:** There is a restaurant at Harvington Hall and a pub in the village.

Harvington Hall

HARVINGTON HALL is a moated Elizabethan manor house (with some medieval parts) owned by the Roman Catholic Archdiocese of Birmingham which contains the best surviving series of priest holes in the country. A fascinating tour will guide you through its history and the various artefacts and items of furniture on view. The property was rescued from dereliction by the Archdiocese in the 1930s and has since undergone an almost continual programme of restoration to capture its essential Tudor and Stuart character.

Open: April to September 11.30am to 5pm Wednesday to Sunday and during March and October at the same times but on Saturday and Sunday only.
Entrance fees: Adults £3.80, senior citizens £3.00; children £2.50, Families £10.50. You could plan to visit either before or after the walk.
Tel: 01562 777846; website: www.harvingtonhall.org.uk.

FROM the Hall walk down the approach lane towards the main road, past part of the moat on your left and, shortly after this point where the lane goes into a left bend, turn off right onto a waymarked track along the edge of a long field. Ignore a waymark right after 100 yards and continue along the field edge and, at the end, go through a gap to stay on line in the next field but now to the right of the boundary hedge. You may have noticed the waymark here informing walkers that they are

104

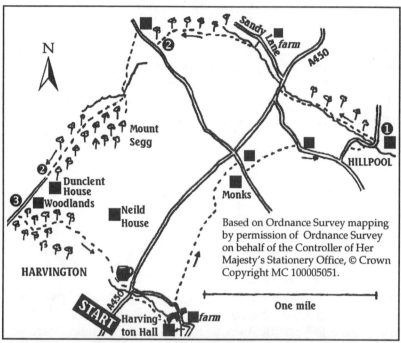

Harvington Hall

on the 'Monarch's Way' – a long distance path which follows the route taken by Charles II on his flight after the battle of Worcester in 1651.

The Clent Hills are in view now ahead right. Ignore a waymark left after some 200 yards and continue along the field edge until about 100 yards from the end of it. Here look carefully for a Monarch's Way waymark on the left leading you down an embankment and across a stile and, once in a pasture field and with your back to the stile, bear half left across it to another waymark visible on the opposite boundary about 120 yards away, to the right of which is a fence stile in the corner. Cross this onto a narrow path between trees and fence before shortly crossing a stile on your left to continue the line forward to the left of an extensive property called 'Monks'. You eventually exit via a stile onto a lane.

Turn right and then left after about 50 yards along a waymarked and surfaced track. Where this swings left after 150 yards, fork right at waymark to go under an electricity pylon and over a stile in a crossing boundary into the adjacent field. At the end cross another stile on your left into an open field. Here you bear slightly right aiming towards a white cottage in the trees and, after a short distance, you will see a stile in the tree line which you cross and descend into a sunken lane.

Turn right on the lane (called Tandy's Lane) and stay on it for about a quarter of a mile before turning left along another lane signed Hillpool. After 100 yards bear right along a public footpath keeping to the right along a wide metalled track. After passing Hilltop Cottage you descend some steps and at the bottom bear left to continue downwards between fences to emerge onto cottage driveway leading to a lane in the hamlet of Hillpool. ❶

Turn right and cross a bridge where the lane swings left. On coming out of the bend turn left onto a narrow path alongside Parkside Cottage. You cross a footbridge before coming out into an attractive meadow bordering a stream. After a while you cross a fence stile to continue ahead between trees and cross another fence stile then another footbridge after 100 yards to follow a rising path. This levels off in a scrubby field where you keep to the top boundary before crossing a stile at the end to stay on the same course in the next field to reach a further stile at which you exit onto the main A450.

Cross the road carefully and turn right to walk along the opposite grass verge for 50 yards before turning off left along Sandy Lane. After passing Fishers Castle Farm the lane goes through a left bend then dips for a short distance. At the bottom of the dip there is a waymarked crossing right of way and you need to go left here down a field track to cross the brook again and continue to a stile where there is a choice of routes. Note the mysterious long abandoned mill building adjacent but please do not enter as the structure is dangerous.

DO NOT CROSS THE STILE – instead turn right in front of it on a path which runs between a fence and the rear of the old mill. Where the track swings left continue ahead on a short path and out into a large field. Walk along the tree lined bottom edge with the brook again below on the right, if you can see it through the trees. After a while ignore a waymark right and continue ahead to pass through a crossing boundary onto a broad stony track. You proceed past two boreholes and go over a stile onto a lane where you turn right. ❷

The lane climbs to Deansford Farm opposite which you bear left along a waymarked bridleway. Keep to the left of the two ways available on a broad sandy track which weaves around a little then swings left over a bridge, immediately after which turn right at a fork along a grassy path at the bottom of the tree line around 'Mount Segg'. The path narrows and continues through pretty woodland and a nature reserve. Please respect the signs and follow the waymarks, eventually crossing a stile onto a driveway to Dunclent House.

Follow the driveway down from Dunclent House and a distance of about 250 yards will bring you to another house called The Woodlands. Immediately after the house, and before reaching a junction, turn off left through a gate (not waymarked at time of research) into a small field. ❸

Cross the field to find a waymarked stile in front of a wood. Having negotiated that follow the narrow path to the left of a post and wire fence which shortly gives way onto a broader path through the wood. This in turn loops left and after a while exits into a field.

Keep to the right of the field boundary but after some 50 yards you need to turn 90 degrees right across the field. You will very shortly pass a waymarked electricity pole to confirm that you are on the right route and Nield Farm is over to your left. At the end of the field you squiggle right then left to continue the same line in the adjoining field until you meet the angle created by hedges to the next field. Now bear right along the top boundary of the same field, go over a stile in a crossing boundary and along a farm track heading towards buildings. After about 100 yards there is a waymark post and here you depart from the track by turning left across a pasture field to join a fence line going towards a road. Exit

In the gardens of Harvington Hall

the field via a stile into the village of Harvington.

If you require refreshment The Dog public house is on your left, otherwise turn right past the lane leading back to the Hall for about 25 yards before going left alongside Forge Cottage on a surfaced driveway. After a few yards go ahead following a waymark along the left edge of a field. Cross a stile at the end of the field and in the next field keep to the left of the boundary fence which takes you to along the other side of the moat passed on the outward route. At the end of the field cross a stile into another field to walk along the left boundary and around the rear of the Hall to return to the car park.

18

Iron Age Malvern – The Herefordshire Beacon

Maps: Landranger 150, Explorer 13.
Start: Car park for the Eastnor Castle Estate on the A438, about two miles east of Eastnor, which itself is two miles east of Ledbury. If you see a telephone kiosk on your right (from the Ledbury direction) you have gone too far. GR 758368.
Distance: 6½ miles – but it may feel like more!
Terrain: Superb hill walking on the southern end of the Malverns with magnificent views and plenty of interest. Some climbing so you will need to be reasonably fit. The area does get crowded at popular times.
Refreshments: There is a public house (Malvern Hills Hotel) at approximately the halfway point and a snack bar nearby.

RETREAT to the main road, cross and turn left along the footpath past the telephone kiosk, a short distance after which the road goes into a right bend. Cross the road again and take the track going off to the left then keep left where the track joins a lane. There are good views to the right along this pleasant leafy lane which runs along the side of the eastern escarpment to Midsummer Hill. After a while you will pass Fairoaks Farm down on the right. Shortly afterwards ignore a turning left and commence a descent. At the base the road loops right over a bridge then starts to climb again and at the top opens out across a common area with a car park entrance directly in front of you.

Pass just to the right of the car park notice and a refuse bin, cross the entrance to the car park and strike off across the common along a relatively faint track almost straight ahead, leaving the road you were on curving away to your right. The path soon becomes more obvious as it gradually loops round to the left and heads towards a wooded area at the base of a hill. When you reach a stone farm track turn left (effectively continuing ahead) and pass through a sparse residential area with paddocks. On arrival at Dales Hall on your right, pass between gateposts either side of the lane and immediately fork gently left along a grassy track. The views get better and better as

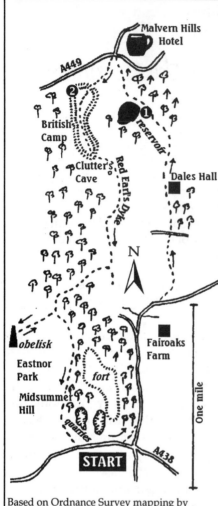

Based on Ordnance Survey mapping by permission of Ordnance Survey on behalf of the Controller of Her Majesty's Stationery Office, © Crown Copyright MC 100005051.

you climb along the base of the tree line and into fringe woodland.

The climb becomes a little more steep as you join a stream on the left but continue onwards to the right of a fenced off area which belongs to Severn Trent Water. When you reach the top you suddenly meet the British Camp Reservoir, although not literally as there is no public access to it. This is the principal source of Great Malvern's water supply and was opened by Princess Mary of Teck in 1895. She later became Queen Mary following her marriage to King George V.

The track turns to tarmac and continues past a cottage and away from the reservoir. Stay on this to reach and cross a large car park which exits onto the main A449. Opposite is the Malvern Hills Hotel where sustenance can be obtained. When ready to resume cross the main road again (or simply turn left on emerging from the car park if not attracted by what is on offer on the other side) to enter on an uphill path signed British Camp. There is an excellent information board here which tells you something about the Malvern Hills and their formation, in particular how the landscape has changed in character over the last 680 million years or so from volcanic to tropical sea to desert through to an Iron Age stronghold in 200BC.

This is a fairly strenuous climb although there are steps to assist in parts. The views get increasingly magnificent the higher you get. At the top you have a superb 360 degree panorama which takes in the Clee Hills, south Shropshire Hills, Brecon Beacons, Cotswolds as well as vast swathes of Herefordshire, Worcestershire, Gloucestershire, etc. **❷**

British Camp is one of the most impressive Iron Age earthworks in Britain and, at its height, over 1000 people would have lived within its 32 acre site area. The lowest rampart is over one mile long and had four entrances. Defensive ditches on the downhill side together with an outer bank made this a formidable barrier against attack. The upper works were built around 200BC and the fort was enlarged just before the Roman invasion. The crowning Citadel is the site of a later Norman castle.

On departure from this spectacular place take the short decorative stone path on the other side of the fort and follow the main way across the Herefordshire Beacon ridge. It loops left and descends quite steeply on another decorative stone path and continues downwards towards the lower ridge in sight. The path then takes a wide swing to the right and passes by a round plinth offering directional guidance to local points of interest.

If you take the lower path from here you will pass a rocky outcrop of volcanic rock into which has been hollowed out a

The Herefordshire Beacon and British Camp

cave. This is called Clutter's Cave and is thought to have been either a hermit's cell or a shepherd's shelter. It may also have been used in connection with sacrificial rituals! The higher path is an earthwork known as Red Earl's Dyke, after Gilbert de Clare the 'Red Earl of Gloucester'. In the Middle Ages the Malverns were a hunting ground and, in 1287, Gilbert built the rampart to stop deer straying across his boundary and not being returned by the neighbouring owner. It is also known as Shire Ditch because it marked the old boundary between Worcestershire and Herefordshire

Continue along the rampart (or rejoin it if walking along the lower path) and start a descent down the main path. Keep right at a fork signed The Gullet and Midsummer Hill and continue along this path for some distance until you come across another round plinth, where you depart from the ridge by turning right. The path descends into a wooded area in the direction of an obelisk which you have been able to see for some time. You reach a junction with the Worcestershire Way and turn left onto it to continue a gradual descent. You arrive at another junction with a choice of routes; you may take the optional extension to visit the obelisk or return to the start directly by going along the path signed Worcestershire Way South, uphill to the half left. If choosing the latter please skip the next paragraph.

View from the Herefordshire Beacon

Those intent upon visiting the obelisk need to go right through a kissing gate. You are immediately confronted by a number of paths radiating out and need to take the second from the left on a gradual incline (the path can get muddy at times) to reach the monument. It was erected in 1812 as a memorial to two local families and is 90ft in height, built of limestone. You are in fact now in Eastnor Park and can see the impressive Eastnor Castle in the middle distance. It is open to the public and is a day out in itself. Return to the turn off point again and bear right onto Worcestershire Way South.

This gravelled path rises past Midsummer Hill, levels off then winds down to the car park and the starting point.

19
Witley Court

Maps: Landranger 138; Explorer 204.
Start: At Witley Court, which is located off the A443 about eleven miles north-west of Worcester and six miles south-west of Stourport-on-Severn and approached via the A451 from that direction. There is a long driveway from the main road to reach the property. GR 769649.
Distance: 5¼ or 6½ miles.
Terrain: Undulating countryside with some climbing up onto Abberley Hill then round to Abberley Hall with its fascinating Clock Tower before returning through the village of Great Witley.
Refreshments: There is a café at Witley Court and pubs in Abberley Village and Great Witley.

EH Witley Court

THESE spectacular ruins are the legacy of unimaginable opulence and wealth once enjoyed by two Black Country families, the Foleys and the Dudleys, whose fortunes were made in ironmaking and mining. The original Jacobean house on the site was transformed into a great Georgian mansion by the Foley family who lived at Witley for 183 years, but their finances were decimated by the 7th Thomas Foley, an obese gambler nicknamed 'Lord Balloon'. In 1837 Witley Court was sold to William Ward, heir to the Dudley fortune, who turned it into one of the most palatial houses in Europe. It was a favourite haunt of many crowned heads, including King Edward VII, and was truly the epitome of elegance and staggering luxury.

It was not to last, however, and when the money supply became depleted in the post-Great War depression, the Court and Estate were sold in 1920. It was purchased by Sir Herbert Smith, a magnate in the carpet industry, and in 1937 on one evening during his absence it caught fire and the skeleton staff were unable to deal with it. Although the fire left most of the property untouched, with the second world war looming, Sir Herbert decided to sell and the estate was split into lots for auction. The building was purchased and subsequently ravaged by demolition contractors. Witley Court's era of greatness ended in neglect and decay until, in 1972, the Department of the Environment, and more latterly, English Heritage took stewardship. Thanks to these bodies considerable preservation work has been carried out and visitors can now picture the grandeur of bygone times at Witley Court.

Open: 1 April to 30 Sept, 10 am to 6 pm; 1 to 31 Oct, 10 am to 5 pm; 1 Nov to 31 Mar, 10am to 4pm Wed-Sun. Closed 24-26 Dec, 1 Jan
Admission: £3.50/ £2.60/ £1.80. Inclusive of audio tour.
Tel: 01299 896636.
It is also possible to visit the superb restored Church adjoining which has an eighteenth century baroque interior by James Gibbs.

WITH your back to Witley Court proceed left along the entrance drive. You will shortly pass some detached houses followed by a fishing pool before continuing along the driveway to exit onto the A443.

Cross directly down a minor road. Over on the left you can see the Clock Tower at Abberley Hall, which is our eventual destination. On reaching the junction with the A451, cross carefully and turn left onto a footpath in front of some houses. After the last house (about 80 yards) turn right onto a waymarked bridleway signed Shavers End, alongside the entrance to Mill Orchards. The path climbs gently to begin with between rows of small trees. You go over a crossing track and after a further 100 yards reach a fork and branch right following a waymark to continue the climb.

Witley Court

Views open up to the rear over the Great Witley area and the way shortly loops left to continue on a steeper course. Continue ahead at waymark on a fairly stiff climb until it levels out at the top. Go over a minor crossing track after which the ground gently falls and you will come to a waymarked junction with the Worcestershire Way. ❶

Turn left onto it and start climbing again before continuing ahead at the next waymark. On a clear day there are excellent views to the left where the Malvern Hills are visible. Keep left at another waymark still following the Worcestershire Way. There are views to the right now although these may be almost totally obscured when the trees are in leaf. Keep following the Worcestershire Way as the path winds and narrows across a ridge. At various points there are super views over Abberley Village and miles beyond, Kidderminster to the half rear, the Clock Tower and numerous farmhouses dotted around in the valley below. You will notice a number of concrete bases in the

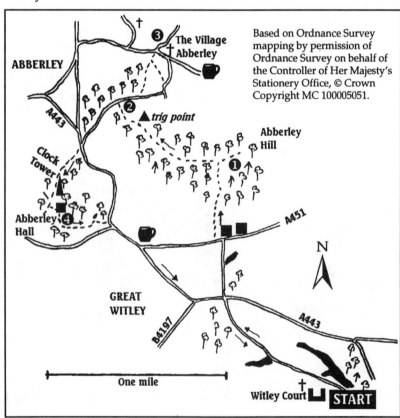

Based on Ordnance Survey mapping by permission of Ordnance Survey on behalf of the Controller of Her Majesty's Stationery Office, © Crown Copyright MC 100005051.

ground with large metal rods attached – these were the anchors for guy ropes to flag poles, the flags being raised and lowered depending upon whether the owners of Abberley Hall were in residence. You pass a trig point and descend to reach a lane where you exit via a fence stile. **②**

There is a choice now depending upon whether you wish to extend the walk by just over a mile to visit the restored Norman church in the village of Abberley. If not wishing to take this option please skip this and the next two paragraphs. Otherwise, turn right onto a steep descent – still the Worcestershire Way, circular walk. Ignore a waymark on the right directing you left into a wood but take note of it because this is where you emerge on return. On arriving at a T-junction turn left still on a descent and, as the lane curves right turn off following a public footpath sign to Abberley Village. You may have to battle for all of five yards through a holly hedge to gain and cross a stile into a field where a well defined path will take you directly across, just to the left of a small wooden barn and more or less towards a church spire. You cross another stile in the field corner and continue to descend in the next field keeping to the right hand boundary. Cross another stile at the bottom to emerge onto a concrete drive. Turn right into the village and, on reaching the road, the church of St. Michael is almost directly in front of you. **③**

The church is tiny and was the original chancel of a larger Norman church. The interior is exquisite, having been restored from its previously decayed state in 1963. On the left is an ancient bell which has been in Abberley since the early sixteenth century and outside is a much earlier relic – a Saxon tomb cover in the 'patio' area which was used by twelfth century builders as a lintel.

After visiting retrace your steps up the driveway opposite and cross the stile into the field traversed on the outward route. However, after only 10 yards, turn right with a waymark across and diagonally up the field to reach a stile in the far fence, just to the left of a cottage. Cross and cut across the edge of the garden to the right of a wooden stable to exit into the adjoining field via another stile. Keep to the right hand boundary and climb for 100 yards before negotiating another stile in a boundary fence. This takes you into a wood and you continue upwards on a well defined path, eventually helped by a flight of wooden steps to emerge onto the lane close to point 2.

Turn right here (those declining to visit the church will have turned left at point 2) and after about a quarter of a mile you arrive at the A443 again. Cross directly on a waymarked bridleway which takes you past the Clock Tower, an ornate sandstone structure with no public access although you can see it quite well. Proceed to a junction in front of the Hall. **4**

Cross the tarmac onto a broad track going away from the buildings. After about 100 yards, at the end of the buildings, there is a waymark which suggests you should continue ahead. Ignore that and instead bear left up a narrower track to skirt around the rear of the property. The track then descends away from it and you pass by some sports pitches on the right before keeping left at a fork. Below right are the remains of a Victorian enclosed garden.

At the bottom of the descent keep right after a pool and go over a gate onto a track alongside private houses. Exit onto the

Abberley Clock Tower

THE Clock Tower was built in 1883/4, is 161 feet high and visible from six counties. Its creator was John Joseph Jones the wealthy owner of the Abberley Estate but the reason why he built the structure is not absolutely certain. One popular theory is that it he constructed the Clock Tower so that none of his numerous workmen and staff should ever have an excuse for not knowing the time! (The clock is by J B Joyce of Whitchurch and the firm still services it). Another, and more likely, reason was to spite his aristocratic rival in Witley Court, Lord Dudley. In Victorian times it had a sewing room with a coal fire, costly hangings and a flushing toilet. During the second war it was used as a Home Guard observation post. Features include the four mosaic clock faces, a sundial and the Jones coat of arms. It is occasionally open to the public.

Abberley Hall itself was once occupied by the Nevilles, one of the country's great baronial families whose fortunes ebbed and flowed with the Yorkist cause in the Wars of the Roses. Following Henry VII's victory at Bosworth in 1485 it was seized as a royal possession then passed to the Walsh family who held it for over 175 years. It was rebuilt in the Italian style by John Moilliet of Geneva in the mid nineteenth century but he died just before work was completed. Towards the end of the same century Joseph Jones acquired it and undertook major alterations in the Victorian manner. It is now a private school.

A443 and cross onto a footpath and turn right. You pass a petrol filling station and after 80 yards cross the road again by the Hundred House pub, at which point fork right on the road through the village of Great Witley. You go past the Post Office and keep going for about half a mile before reaching the driveway back to Witley Court.

Abberley Clock Tower

20

Broadway

Maps: Outdoor Leisure 45 – The Cotswolds.

Start : From the Dover's Hill car park, about two miles to the north-west of Chipping Campden. Take the road out from the west end of the village (Dyer's Lane) towards Broadway and at a crossroads go straight across to find the car park shortly on your right. From the Broadway direction you need to turn left off the A44 towards Chipping Campden and follow a minor road for about two miles before turning left to Dover's Hill. GR 136396.

Distance: 7¾ miles.

Terrain: Scenic hill country on the northern edge of the Cotswolds taking in two areas of outstanding natural beauty owned by the National Trust, a curious hill top folly and the picturesque town of Broadway. Some steepish climbs, particularly on the section up to Broadway Tower.

Refreshments: Plenty of establishments in Broadway and there is a restaurant at Broadway Tower.

From the car park there is a short walk to the spectacular viewpoint at Dover's Hill and a topograph describing the distant landmarks visible on a clear day. The hill takes its name from a local barrister, Robert Dover, who initiated a festival of sport and pageantry in 1612 which was called the 'Cotswold Olimpicks' centuries before the modern Olympics were started. The tradition is maintained to this day with the games still being held in the spring. The topograph is dedicated to Frederick Griggs who, together with historian G M Trevelyan, purchased the property to save it from hotel development and presented it to the National Trust in 1929, since when it has been open to the public. The property is rich in flora and fauna and there is waymarked trail and other paths around it.

WHEN ready to start turn left (facing the topograph) down a gulley, past a marker post and through a kissing gate by the National Trust sign turning right onto a descending lane. After about 200 yards look carefully for a waymarked fence stile in the hedge on your left under an ash tree before reaching farm buildings. Cross into a pasture field and walk parallel to the right hedged boundary and take in the

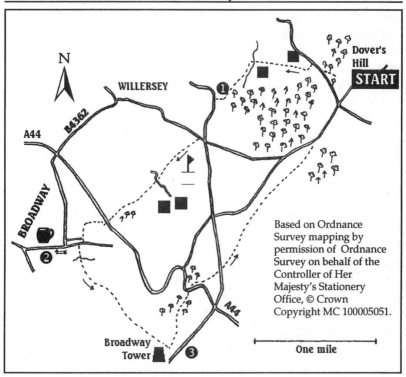

extensive views from here across to the Malvern, Clee and Clent Hills which were not so easily visible from Dover's Hill due to the intervention of trees. You pass a marker post and, at the end of the field, go through a gate then directly across and down another pasture field to a double stile on the far side about 100 yards away.

Cross the stile and continue ahead though very slightly to the left across a ridged field and on the far side you dip down to a stile in the far boundary, which is not visible until you are almost there. These ridges are the remnants of a medieval form of soil cultivation known as 'ridge and furrow'. A horse would pull a single plough moving the soil out of the furrow and depositing it as a ridge alongside. When the system was no longer used the soil grassed over leaving the ridges which are still evident today. Having negotiated the stile continue the descent in the next field, gradually moving away from the left boundary to drop down to a farm track about 40 yards to the right of a stone cottage.

Go over the track and continue the line forward in the adjacent field to reach the top left corner where you will find two footbridges hidden in the trees. Take the one right in the corner and over a stile out into the next field where you follow the left boundary of trees for about 80 yards before crossing another stile adjacent to a gate onto a broader track where there is a somewhat complicated choice of routes. Go ahead over a bridge to reach a second stile literally only a few yards further on BUT DO NOT CROSS – instead bear left in front of it on a broad rising track which runs parallel to the lower track for a short distance before curving away along the right edge of a wood. This track, known as Buckle Street, can get muddy at times and climbs steadily before leveling out and looping right to exit onto a lane. **❶**

Turn left on the lane to re-start the ascent and after about a third of a mile you reach a crossroads, where you bear right towards Willersey. A distance of only 50 yards will bring you to a left turn along a waymarked bridleway which follows the edge of a golf course. Again there are superb views along this section across the Vale of Evesham towards the hills identified earlier. The village of Willersey is also in view down below on the right. After a while the path opens out onto part of the golf course and you continue ahead staying close to the fence until the way diverts behind a hedge screen then loops left to reach a gateway. Go through the gap alongside to join a track leading down to meet the driveway to the golf club.

Cross the driveway directly and continue on the downward track with Broadway now well in sight ahead. The track peters out but continue on the same line passing to the left of a line of scrubby trees down to a waymark post which you can see ahead. Go forward here and through a wicket gate before bearing slightly right to follow the obvious route towards the main road (A44). Before you reach it you go through a waymarked gate on the right, down an embankment and through another gate along an underpass to the main road. You will go through a further gate on the other side of the underpass and bear right across a stile by another gate onto a wide stony track.

After only a few yards you cross a fence stile by a gate on your left into a field where you follow the left boundary. At the end of the field cross another fence stile and turn right onto a path between trees and fence. You soon exit via a kissing gate onto a residential road and cross this directly onto another path running behind houses. The surface turns to tarmac and emerges at the end of a cul-de-sac where you go ahead on another tarmac

Broadway

BROADWAY is one of the best known and attractive of the Cotswold Towns. The main street is an ancient 'ridgeway' and was on the main road from Worcester to London, hence the name 'broadway'. You can spend hours just looking into the shops and numerous places of interest or visit the Tourist Information Office for specific details. One of the most fascinating buildings is the Lygon Arms which is steeped in history and played host to both Charles I and Oliver Cromwell.

footpath between stone walls. On reaching the High Street turn right into the centre of Broadway. **❷**

On departing walk back along the main street past Leamington Road for about 250 yards then branch off right onto the Cotswold Way along a stone driveway between houses. Cross a fence stile and continue ahead over another stile 40 yards further on and into a pasture field where you stay on the same line parallel with the left boundary. You need to negotiate a small brook in a crossing boundary then continue the line ahead to the top corner of the next field where there is another fence stile to cross before bearing half left on the obvious path across the adjoining field. There is a marker post in the middle of the field to guide you.

In a crossing boundary is another marker post presenting a choice of routes – take the option more or less straight ahead to the next crossing boundary which is only about 50 yards further on. Cross a stile here and stay on the same line following the waymark (you have now entered National Trust territory again and what was previously a gradual climb now starts to get rather more noticeable) passing another marker post guiding you to the top right corner of a field. Cross another stile and continue onwards and upwards to the right of a dry stone wall to reach the top of the incline where there is a seat for you to take a breather and admire the magnificent views over Broadway and the Vale of Evesham.

Regrettably the climb has not quite finished and you cross what is a rather odd stile, which is bit like a hybrid between a fence and a stile, then another a little further on to stay on the same course across several more fields before the ground levels out and Broadway Tower comes into view. You cross a stile onto a path between fences which leads up to the Tower. ❸

On leaving return to the path and go through the waymarked gate opposite on a path across undulating ground before negotiating a kissing gate into an open pasture field. Continue the line forward past a waymark post leading you down a gulley to another waymark post. You are led into a wooded area and cross a stile after which go straight on until bearing right at a fork by the next waymark following the Cotswold Way sign. At the next waymark you bear round to the right parallel with the A44 below and turn left onto a track by a

Broadway Tower

Broadway Tower

BROADWAY TOWER is a folly built in the late eighteenth century and is well worth a visit. It is situated on a Beacon site which at, 1024 feet, is the second highest point in the Cotswolds. The use of the point as a beacon site originates from the days when fires were relied upon for communication and was one of a chain that celebrated the Queens Jubilee in 1977.

There are differing theories as to the purpose of the Tower's construction but it was created during the great eighteenth century fad for folly building and was designed by James Wyatt, who also built the palace at Kew. It has a colourful history and has strong associations with William Morris, the fabric designer. There are interesting archives and exhibitions in the building which go into some detail about its history and its owners. Views from the top are marvellous and cover thirteen counties.

stone quarry but stay on it for a few yards before turning left again along a narrow path down to the main road.

Cross the road carefully and at the choice of routes on the other side continue on the Cotswold Way through a picnic area and past another topograph, immediately after which turn left at a waymark over a stile into a field. Bear half right diagonally across the field on a worn path to reach a lane which you cross to stay on the Cotswold Way. You go diagonally across the next field and through a gap in a dry stone wall into the next just cutting off the right corner to pass through another section of dry stone wall on your right about 150 yards ahead.

You are now on a broad grassy swathe between lines of trees which is known as The Mile Drive. You stay on this for some time – for about a mile in fact – and at the end you are funnelled onto a path through a small spinney and round to a step stile by a lane. Cross onto the lane and turn right and, after a third of a mile, turn left at crossroads to regain the start after another 250 yards or so.

21

Kenilworth Castle

Maps: Landranger 139 & 140; Pathfinder 955; Explorer 221.
Start: From the main Castle car park to the south or the smaller car park on the north side almost opposite the Queen & Castle Public House. The town of Kenilworth is situated off the A46 to the south of Coventry and to the north of Warwick. Once you are there just follow the direction signs to the Castle. GR 278723.
Distance: 4 or 5½ miles.
Terrain: Easy walking along well used paths in countryside to the west of the Castle with an optional but well worthwhile diversion to the exquisite church in the village of Honiley.
Refreshments: Plenty of places in Kenilworth Town.

EH   Kenilworth Castle

THE great sandstone castle of Kenilworth is one of the finest and most extensive ruins in England and was the fortress of kings and nobles for more than 800 years. Built during the reign of Henry I in the twelfth century, it became one of the greatest strongholds in the land and the centrepiece of many events which shaped the course of history.

One of four castles handed to the barons under the terms of the Magna Carta (although King John never actually surrendered it), Kenilworth was the headquarters of Simon de Montfort during his revolt against Henry III in the mid thirteenth century, the scene of Edward II's abdication in 1326 and, during the latter part of that century, it was held by the great John of Gaunt who carried out major improvements including the resplendent Great Hall.

The mid-fifteenth century saw Kenilworth become the home of Robert Dudley, Earl of Leicester and favourite of Queen Elizabeth I and thus started the last significant phase of the Castle's history. In 1575 the Queen visited the Castle and was entertained in lavish and splendid style. She stayed for nineteen days during which 190 oxen were roasted and 45,000 gallons of beer and wine consumed. The occasion was immortalised in Sir Walter Scott's novel *Kenilworth*.

In the Civil War the Castle was partially destroyed and subsequently passed through a number of ownerships before being placed in Official care in 1937.

Open: 1 April to 30 Sept, 10 am to 6 pm; 1 to 31 Oct, 10 am to 5 pm;
1 Nov to 31 Mar, 10am to 4pm.
Admission: £3.50/ £2.60/ £1.80.Audio tour available.

FROM the entrance you need to skirt around the south and east sides of the Castle along the line of the former moat. To do this leave the Castle precincts via the entrance causeway then almost immediately branch off right through a kissing gate to follow the line of the old moat around the edge. You arrive at a pretty thatched cottage and continue forward on a grassed area to the left of it to reach a squeeze stile, which you negotiate before turning left onto a broad stone track.

Ignore a footpath right after 120 yards and, as you continue along the track, imagine the fields on your left covered in a huge lake. *This is the site of Kenilworth Great Pool which spread over an area of 150 acres and was half a mile long. As well as playing a strategic role in defence of the Castle, it would also have been used for recreational purposes. Picture the scene during the visit of Elizabeth to Lord Robert Dudley – the Pool must have been a panoply of sail and colour with a myriad boats plying up and down in a noisy feast of royal entertainment.*

At 'Hollyfast' fork right onto a grassy track (before reaching farmyard) which winds between rows of small trees to emerge at a stile. Cross then go immediately over a stone driveway and through a field towards an area of raised ground. *This is the site of*

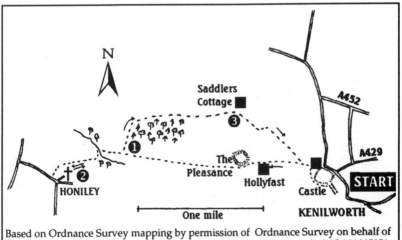

Based on Ordnance Survey mapping by permission of Ordnance Survey on behalf of the Controller of Her Majesty's Stationery Office, © Crown Copyright MC 100005051.

Kenilworth Castle

'The Pleasance' – a summer lodge built by King Henry V, accessed by boat from the Great Pool and surrounded by two concentric moats which can be clearly seen. The building was used by various royal personages for more 'intimate' occasions or when they simply wished to escape from the grandeur of the state apartments. It was demolished by Henry VIII.

Go to the left of the Pleasance to reach a stile next to a gate in the crossing boundary ahead. Cross the stile and follow the same line forward but now with the hedge on your right. At the end of the field you cross a footbridge and stile to continue on the path along the field edge. This *was* the corner of Chase Wood but the trees have been cut back and the wood now runs parallel some way off to the right. At the end of the second long field you reach a stone crossing track. **❶**

The way is right although you can if you wish (and I can highly recommend that you do) take a diversion to visit the village of Honiley and its exquisite church. The following directions take you there but please make careful note of the route as you will need to backtrack to point 1 afterwards. Cross the track directly and continue forward to the left of a hedge. At the end of the field bear round to the left to a footbridge and waymark, cross into another field with a brook and trees on the left and follow the waymark as the path takes you in the direction of the church and then to the right of it. At the end of the field, you cross a stile and turn left. After a further 40 yards cross another stile to continue through the centre of the following field before crossing yet another stile and a footbridge onto a lane. Turn left and left again after a few yards up to the church. **2**

The church of St. John Baptist was built in the early eighteenth century and remains largely unaltered to present day. It is beautifully finished in baroque style and has numerous interesting features including boxed pews, a gallery supported by

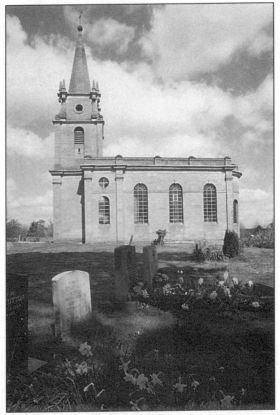

Honiley Church

fluted marble columns, black and white marble floor and stained glass. There is a booklet available inside the church with more detailed descriptions and history.

Now retrace your steps back to the crossing track at point 1 and turn left onto a broad stony track which takes you along the east end of Chase Wood. If you did not visit the church you will have turned right at this point as indicated earlier. At the end of the wood bear right onto a tarmac lane alongside the north side of it. You will stay on this for getting on for a mile. After passing the entrance to Pleasance Farm you shortly arrive at Saddlers Cottage, at the end of which is a waymarked crossing right of way. **3**

Take the stile on the right into a field and head across it towards the Castle in the distance following a walked path. Go over a stile in a crossing boundary and continue the line forward over the next field to cross a further stile and turn left. After

129

another 30 yards there is yet another stile to cross into a large field with the Castle now well in view. There is a well trodden path across this field and on the other side you go over a further stile and continue forward over the next field. Go through a gate and across the next field and over the last stile onto a broad stony track. Now simply reverse steps back to the start.

22

Edge Hill

Maps: Landranger 151; Pathfinder 1021; Explorer 205.

Start: At Upton House (National Trust) which is located just off the A422, about 14 miles south-west of Stratford-upon-Avon and 11 miles north-east of Shipston-on-Stour. The village of Edgehill is 1¼ miles to the north. GR 370456.

Please note that Upton House does not open until 2pm (see below) and I would suggest that your visit is undertaken at the end of the walk. The National Trust have indicated that, providing a visit to the house *is* intended, they would have no objection to walkers using the car park outside of normal opening hours but would appreciate a telephone call in advance on 01295 670266 so that they know, for security reasons, who is on the property. This may not apply when a planned new restaurant is completed as it will be open in the morning – but a telephone call would be advisable to check the position. If you do not intend to visit the house there is a lay-by just around the corner to the west of the house at point 3 on the walk plan. GR 363458.

Distance: 5 miles.

Terrain: Farmland to start before reaching the picturesque village of Ratley, followed by a ramble across the escarpment of Edge Hill, overlooking the famous Civil War battle site and finishing with a look at Upton House, a remodelled seventeenth century residence with a unique exhibition. Some fields may be cropped in summer, particularly those early on in the walk.

Refreshments: There is an excellent pub in Ratley – the Rose and Crown reputedly established in 1098! – and the Castle Inn at Edge Hill, which is an experience in itself.

THE first section of this walk involves some road walking and crossing farmland which, without wishing to be unkind, is not the most attractive I have ever seen. But, be patient!

If starting from the lay-by at point 3, you will need to turn right in an easterly direction and follow the instructions in the last two paragraphs and continue on past the entrance to Upton House before picking up the route from the following paragraph. If starting from the house retreat back down the driveway to the A422 and turn right.

Stay on the main road for about a third of a mile before turning left along a lane signed Hornton and Horley – there is a grass verge along the main road to make things a little easier. However, you will no doubt be pleased to get off it and continue along the lane passing a Cotswold stone cottage and a British Telecom station, both on the right. Shortly after this point, as the lane goes into a right bend, turn left down a waymarked path into a field.

Follow the hedged boundary on your right (could be cropped up to the edge in summer) to the end where you continue ahead along a path running between trees. The path goes to the right of farm buildings and emerges by a stile and gate at the rear of them. Cross the stile into an 'agricultural graveyard' to the right of Uplands Farmhouse and stay ahead with a post &

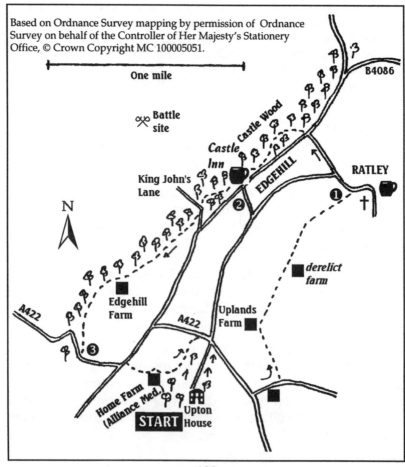

One mile

B4086

Battle site

Castle Wood

Castle Inn

EDGEHILL

RATLEY

King John's Lane

N

derelict farm

Edgehill Farm

A422

A422

Uplands Farm

Home Farm (Alliance Med.)

Upton House

START

wire fence on your right. After 50 yards or so, where the fence turns 90 degrees right, bear less sharply right to join a farm track leading downhill. This takes you through a waymarked gate and forward along the track in a large field heading in the direction of some curious derelict farm buildings.

The track becomes less well defined but stay with the line of it as you descend then rise steeply to the left of the derelict buildings. It is possible that passage may be more difficult when the field is cropped. After a stiff climb you proceed into the next field to the right of the boundary hedge. After about 100 yards, before getting to the end of the field, go through a gate on your left then turn immediately right over a waymarked stile. There is a corrugated building on your left now as you walk through a narrow pasture field between fenced boundaries. You are effectively following the same line as before but on the other side of the boundary. The right boundary bears around to the right and as it continues to do so you head off diagonally downhill towards the village of Ratley and in the bottom right corner of the field cross a stile onto a farm track. Follow the track round between farm buildings to go through a number of gates before emerging on a lane in the village. **❶**

The way is left but a right turn is recommended to visit the attractive Cotswold Stone village scene. You pass the Old Post Office and the church of St. Peter ad Vincula, an interesting building with a thirteenth century 'preaching cross' in the churchyard. The dedication *ad Vincula* is rare and means 'in chains' (at the gates of Rome). If the thought of refreshment at this stage is tempting, the Rose and Crown should fit the bill. The sign outside announces that it is reputed to have been established in 1098 – obviously an earlier building, but did they have public alehouses then?

Reverse your steps up through the village and continue on the lane (Church Street) which is quite steep. You pass a row of cottages and continue ahead at a crossroads before meeting the B4086 after another 300 yards. Turn left then immediately right down a waymarked path into Castle Wood. You descend steps on the Centenary Way path (Jacobs Ladder). Beware, the way could be slippery in wet weather. Continue the descent to the bottom of the tree line where there is a waymark post, beyond which you can look out across the ground upon which was fought the battle of Edge Hill in 1642. There is an information panel here (English Heritage) providing details of a permissive route around the base of the hill, which you could do as an optional extra if you wish. Unfortunately, access to the battle site itself is not permitted as it forms part of Ministry of Defence land.

The Battle of Edge Hill

ON Sunday 23rd October 1642, King Charles gathered his troops at the top of the hill behind you in preparation for the first major battle of the English Civil War and also one of the fiercest. The Parliamentary forces under Lord Essex, having marched from Worcester in ten days, were arranged in the plain below beyond the village of Radway. Many local families were involved and, symptomatic of Civil Wars, father fought son and brother took arms against brother. All together about 30,000 men fought on that day and some 10% of them died.

The Royalists charged down the hill to meet the Roundheads and a bloody fight ensued into the evening when darkness brought a halt to the encounter. The outcome was inconclusive and both armies withdrew – the Parliamentarians to Kineton and the Royalists back to Edge Hill. There are many tales of ghostly hauntings around the battle site; the cavalry charging down the hill with their heads under their arms, travellers being jostled as if in a crowd of long dead soldiers, a cottage where blood seeps through the ceiling to the floor beneath...shall we continue with the walk now?

Turn left in front of the waymark post along a broader path. Enjoy a pleasant walk through fringe woodland and, on reaching another waymark post at a fork, take the left option uphill. At the top of the rise go through a gate into the car park of the Castle Inn. This really is a splendid place to stop for refreshments, particularly on a good day when you can enjoy the panoramic view across the battlefield and the South Warwickshire countryside. Indeed, on a clear day the view is reputed to embrace twelve counties. The octagonal tower was opened in 1750 and was based upon Guy's tower at Warwick Castle. It is said that the tower marks the spot where King Charles raised his standard before the battle. ❷

When ready to depart, retrace your steps to the footpath at the rear of the inn but don't follow the inward path. Instead turn left following the waymark (also downhill) along and round to the rear of the property. The surface turns from concrete to earth and descends to the base of the hill again where you turn left at a junction. The path twists through trees, rising to continue along the top of the escarpment through very attractive woodland. You pass a line of old beech trees and come to a junction, where you bear left although effectively continuing ahead. This is the top of King John's Lane and probably existed at the time of the battle being the old road from Kineton to Radway. According to local legend King Charles escaped capture while watching the battle from the nearby mound known as King's Clump.

After only 20 yards on King John's Lane, and before it joins up with the road, turn right at a waymark to follow a narrow path along the top of the tree line. Continue along here until you reach a junction with a narrow tarmac lane and turn left onto it. The lane goes up to Edgehill Farm but after a few yards, and before reaching the farm buildings, bear right to continue on a narrow path through woodland. Take care though – you want the second of two paths close together and not the one going downhill on a concrete surface. The path takes you to the rear of the farm buildings and can be nettly in summer. Eventually it

exits onto a road after about half a mile where you turn left. After a few yards those starting from the lay-by will re-gain their vehicles. ❸

Those who started from Upton will continue on the main road as it swings left and but after only another 20 yards turn right down a broad waymarked farm track. After 150 yards the track swings left through a gate towards a farm. You arrive at

The Castle Inn

a waymarked gate in front of the buildings, which in fact turn out to be a medical research establishment (Alliance Medical Ltd.). The waymark and O.S. plan direct you left across the car park and to the rear of the buildings but, with the approval of the owners of the property and the adjacent field, it is much easier to stay outside the perimeter fence. So, turn left at the gate and follow the fence round the corner of the property.

You will come to a double width gate waymarked back in the opposite direction across the property – at this point leave the boundary on a line half left up a grassy bank to another gate in the opposite boundary. This leads into a small paddock with a further gate in only 10 yards or so. Go through this and stay close to the left side post and wire fence to proceed through a long pasture. You pass a hollow on your right with hawthorn bushes in it, and immediately after this your line leaves the fence to cross the pasture diagonally right into the far corner. Here you will find a waymarked stile which you cross onto the A422 and turn right past the entrance drive to Home Farm and after a further 50 yards turn right again at the entrance to Upton House.

Upton House · NT

UPTON HOUSE was built of local stone in 1695 and remodelled in 1927. As well as outstanding collections of old masters, Brussels tapestries, Sevres porcelain and Chelsea figures the house also has a superb exhibition of paintings and posters commissioned by Shell between 1921 and 1946 when the second Viscount Bearsted, who gave the property to the National Trust, was Chairman of the Company. The gardens are superb and hold the National Collection of Asters.

Open (2001) 31 March to 31 Oct, daily except Thur & Fri. 1-5 pm
Admission £5.50; family £13.75. Garden only £2.70

Gloucestershire

23
Hailes Abbey

Maps: Outdoor Leisure 45 – The Cotswolds.
Start: The car park at Hailes Abbey,which is situated about two miles to the north-east of Winchcombe and approached via a minor road off the B4362. GR 051300.
Distance: 8 miles.
Terrain: Rolling countryside on the edge of the Cotswolds with some excellent views. Plenty of interest and incorporating a visit to the picturesque town of Winchcombe. This is a fairly long walk with a lot to see, so please do plan carefully. A whole day is required to do it justice. A little climbing is involved but nothing too taxing.
Refreshments: Plenty in Winchcombe. There is also a tea room just after the start of the walk.

EH Hailes Abbey

HAILES ABBEY was built in the thirteenth century by Richard, Earl of Cornwall and was one of the last Cistercian houses to be founded in England. It owes its existence to a pledge given by Richard during a perilous sea voyage that, if he survived, he would found a religious house and he was aided in this by his brother, King Henry III, who gave him the manor of Hailes.

It later passed to his son, Edmund, who gave the resident monks a phial said to contain the blood of Christ and thus Hailes became one of the great medieval pilgrimage abbeys. It remained so until the dissolution when the phial was removed to London and declared to be 'honey clarified and coloured with saffron'. The Abbey survived the dissolution in part (see note at point 1 below) and indeed was occupied as two farmhouses in the early seventeenth century but later fell into ruin until its donation to the National Trust. It is now in the care of English Heritage.

Open: 1 April to 30 Sept, 10 am to 6 pm; 1 to 31 Oct, 10 am to 5 pm; 1 Nov to 31 Mar, 10am to 4pm Sat-Sun. Closed 24-26 Dec, 1 Jan
Admission: £2.60/ £2.00/ £1.30.Audio tour included.

YOU will need to decide whether to visit the Abbey before or after the walk – I would advise the former just in case you are detained en route by other things of interest and fail to leave sufficient time – at least one hour will be required. On leaving turn right along the lane and, where it curves right towards the Orchard Tea Room, continue ahead on a stony track marked Cotswold Way into fringe woodland. The track rises gradually and curves around the edge of Hailes Wood. About 100 yards after the wood ends there is a waymarked crossroads of paths and you go left over a stile waymarked Beckbury Camp and still on the Cotswold Way. Having crossed the stile you proceed half left up the centre of the field but veering towards the left side of it aiming for the belt of trees on the far left boundary where, to the right, you will find a waymarked gate. The Malvern Hills are visible now in the distance over to your left.

Go through the gate and continue the line across the next section of field and through another gate in a crossing boundary about 100 yards ahead. Stay on the line over undulating ground towards a ridge surmounted by a monument, at the base of which is a waymark. Here bear round to the right and, after a stiffish climb, you will reach the monument. ❶

The Cotswold stone monument is intriguing as there are no clues as to its purpose. A little local research reveals that it was erected by a nineteenth century owner of the Stanway Estate and appar-

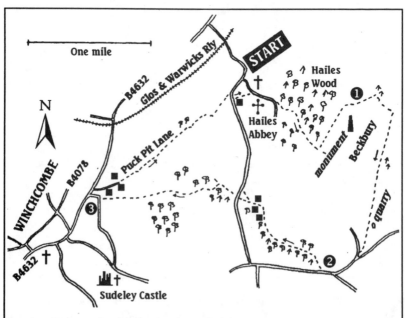

ently marks the spot where Thomas Cromwell watched Hailes Abbey burn in 1539 as part of Henry VIII's dissolution. The ridge itself is part of the Iron Age hill fort known as Beckbury Camp.

Go through the gateway at the rear of the monument and walk the left boundary of a field along the top of part of the earthworks, with tremendous views to the left over the Vale of Evesham. You go through a gate in a crossing boundary and proceed to the end of the next field where you turn right as waymarked to continue with a stone wall on your left. On reaching a gate on

Monument at Beckbury

the left, go through and ahead but now with the wall on your right. Continue the line on a stony farm track and, on reaching a crossing track after 80 yards, turn right onto it. After about 300 yards, as the path goes into a left hand bend, continue straight ahead to follow the waymark around a gate onto a narrower path. This soon broadens out and you find that you are fairly enclosed by trees on both sides.

You come out of the trees and shortly ignore a waymark right. After a further third of a mile or so you will pass by a former stone quarry on the left and eventually exit via a gate onto a metalled lane where you continue the line ahead and bear right along the lane signposted Winchcombe. At a T-junction bear right then immediately on your right there are two waymark posts close together. Take the second one through a gate onto a stony farm track. ❷

Follow the track past a metal barn and through a waymarked gate to continue on the track to the right of a belt of mixed trees. After about 120 yards, just before the track dips, fork left through another waymarked gate (Gloucestershire Way) into fringe woodland although you soon emerge into pasture via yet another gate. Keep to the obvious route to the right of the tree line and, after a while go over a stile heading towards a farm in view. A waymarked gate in front of the farm buildings directs you 90 degrees right alongside a post and wire fence and you follow this round through a gate to the left of the farmhouse, after which you bear right onto a concrete farm track alongside farm buildings. You will shortly arrive at a waymark by a cattle grid where there is a choice of routes.

If you would prefer to cut short the walk at this stage take the right option which takes you out onto a lane and bear right to follow it for about three quarters of a mile back to Hailes. Otherwise, go left onto a broad stony track and on reaching a lane cross it directly through a waymarked gate, then go straight over a pasture field to a stile in a crossing boundary 100 yards or so ahead. You still have magnificent views over to the right and, from time to time during the summer, you may hear the sounds of the Gloucestershire and Warwickshire Steam Railway which runs close by.

Cross the stile and the next field on the same line to a gate on the opposite boundary where the town of Winchcombe comes into view below. There is another choice here and you need to go left over some fairly rough and steep ground up to a waymarked stile. Cross this onto a narrow rising path between trees and, after crossing another stile, the path descends quite steeply through bracken and undergrowth so please take extra care on this section. The ground levels off as you cross a waymarked fence to follow a narrow grassy path between bracken which is shortly joined by a post and wire fence on your right. Stay with this until arriving at a waymarked gate on your right.

Once through the gate bear half left downwards and fairly steeply so, again take care as it can get slippy at times. There are steps to assist in parts. Keep following the waymark post as you emerge into more open and undulating terrain to go through a kissing gate under a willow tree. Continue downwards through the next pasture field and at the bottom go through another kissing gate in a crossing boundary and then a third at the end of

Winchcombe

THE Cotswold town of Winchcombe has its roots in Neolithic times as there is an impressive long barrow at Belas Knap nearby. There is also considerable evidence of Roman and Saxon habitation. In the Middle Ages it was a flourishing trading centre assisted by the flow of pilgrims to the Abbey and the shrine of the murdered boy prince, St. Kenelm.

The Abbey was destroyed during the Dissolution and the town went into decline until the early seventeenth century when home grown tobacco revived its fortunes even though cultivation of the crop was in defiance of authority. Today numerous visitors are attracted here and to the many places of interest nearby, including Hailes Abbey and the spectacular, atmospheric Sudeley Castle.

the following small field. This leads you onto a metalled track where you turn right. Turn right again when you reach a junction with a lane which takes you down to meet the B4632. If wishing to visit Winchcombe (recommended) turn left, otherwise turn right. ❸

Return to the point of egress onto the B4632 and walk past it for about 100 yards before turning right down Puck Pit Lane. After passing some properties the lane degenerates into a broad stony track which itself ends at a stile between gates. Cross this onto a narrow path between fence and hedge and then another stile into a pasture field. Bear slightly left away from the right boundary of trees more or less crossing the field diagonally to the end of another line of trees coming in from the left. Underneath the last tree is a footbridge which is crossed before proceeding directly across the next field about 40 yards away from the right boundary.

Go though a kissing gate in a crossing boundary and continue the line forward across a larger field heading for another kissing gate in front of a clump of trees on the far side. This takes you around the corner of the adjacent field and over a stile into another field which you cross directly to the opposite boundary. Now turn right along this opposite boundary and at the end go through an opening onto a broad stony track. Turn left and continue through to meet a lane.

Turn right on the lane and, after about 120 yards, bear left with the Cotswold Way sign along a track adjacent to a house called 'The Barn' and through a waymarked gate into a field. Keep the same line across it to go through a gap between two groups of trees. In this field is an ancient stone, which local information suggests found its way there during the Dissolution. Proceed forward to a gate in the corner which leads you back to the start.

If you have time do visit Hailes Church opposite – it is a truly remarkable building dating from the twelfth century and containing some fascinating Medieval wall paintings which have recently been scientifically treated. There is an 'Ode to Boots' posted on the entrance door which is perhaps the politest way imaginable of asking visitors to take off muddy footwear!

Hailes Abbey

24

Odda and Tewkesbury

Maps: Explorer 14 (mainly) and 179.
Start: At Odda's Chapel in the village of Deerhurst, about four miles south-west of Tewkesbury by road. Take the A38 Gloucester Road out of the City and after getting on for three miles turn right along the B4213, then fork off right after another half a mile to Deerhurst. The chapel is signposted and there is a small car park opposite for which a modest charge is made by honesty box. GR 869298. If you prefer the walk could be started from Tewkesbury.
Distance: 6½ miles.
Terrain: A gentle walk loaded with history, starting with a Saxon chapel followed by a wander along the banks of the River Severn into Tewkesbury via the 1471 Wars of the Roses battle trail. Visit the splendid Tewkesbury Abbey and whatever else you wish to see in this ancient city before returning through farmland to finish with a look at the evocative church in Deerhurst.
Refreshments: Plenty in Tewkesbury.

EH   ## Odda's Chapel

EARL ODDA was a kinsman of Edward the Confessor and held sway for a time over a large part of south-west England. The Chapel, which survives largely intact, was erected in memory of his brother Elfric who died in 1053, only three years before Odda himself. Odda was a pious man and it is likely that the chapel was used as an oratory, or chantry chapel, and served from the nearby monastery, which is now the parish church.

Following the death of Edward the Confessor in 1066 the chapel was granted to the Abbey of Westminster in whose ownership it remained for centuries. At some point it was secularised and incorporated into Abbot's Court which it adjoins. The chapel had a dedication stone, which was found in a nearby orchard in 1675 but it was not until 1885 that it was recognised as the building referred in the dedication inscription. It was subsequently restored to its original condition, or as near to it as is known.

Open: 1 April to 30 Sept, 10 am to 6 pm; 1 to 31 Mar, 10am to 4pm. Closed 24-26 Dec, 1 Jan.
Entry free.

Based on Ordnance Survey mapping by permission of Ordnance Survey on behalf of the Controller of Her Majesty's Stationery Office, © Crown Copyright MC 100005051.

Odda's Chapel

ALMOST opposite the chapel go through a waymarked gate onto a broad stony track and after about 150 yards turn right along the bank of the River Severn. You will walk alongside the river for some time, passing through a gate and crossing a stile. Judging by the water level marker posts this is flood plain, so perhaps I should issue a warning not to attempt this walk during periods of excessive rainfall! Where the path curves right towards a gate in front of a wood continue ahead along the river bank before passing through a gate leading to the Cheltenham College boathouse. On the other side of the boathouse go through another gate onto a tarmac lane. Ignore a waymark shortly on your right but make a note of it as you will need to pick it up (not literally) on the return leg.

You come to a sewage works on your right and, after a further 250 yards, look carefully for a waymark, also on your right, bearing crossed swords and a rose. This is the start of the trail laid out by Tewkesbury Council around the site of the great battle fought here in 1471. Follow the waymark and shortly cross a stile on your right and keep to the right of a hedge line as you walk through a meadow. At the end, just before exiting onto a lane you will find an information board giving background history to the battle and details of the protagonists. **❶**

At the information board you look back along the way you have just walked and discover it is called 'Bloody Meadow'. It is not difficult to imagine the origin for the name and, at the time of my research, this was given added poignancy by the fact that the meadow contained a profusion of red and white may trees flowering next to each other.

Behind the information board go through a kissing gate before turning right on a lane leading towards the golf club. After only 50 yards turn left with the battle waymark along another lane then immediately depart from it over a stile on your left into a field. Follow the right boundary and at some point – it may be most convenient at the top end – you need to move over to the left side in order to cross a footbridge (but ignore the footbridge about 100 yards before the end of the field). This leads out onto a tarmac path where you turn right alongside some houses before crossing another footbridge and stile into a field. Turn left here with the battle waymark, right through Edward of York's lines, and at the top cross a waymarked stile onto the A38 and turn right.

The Battle of Tewkesbury

THE battle of Tewkesbury was one of the fiercest engagements of the Wars of the Roses and resulted in a terrible defeat for the Lancastrians, led by Margaret of Anjou (queen of the imprisoned Henry VI) and Edward of Lancaster, Prince of Wales. Edward was killed in the battle and he, together with many of his followers, are buried in Tewkesbury Abbey. Margaret fled to Malvern but was captured a few days later and sent to the Tower of London to await ransom by the king of France. Henry was put to death in the same place. The victorious Yorkists, including Richard of Gloucester, later to become Richard III, suffered their own reversal in the next battle in the Wars of the Roses at Bosworth Field in 1485.

It would be advisable to cross onto the footpath but you only need to endure the main road conditions for about 200 yards as you take the first turning off on the left, called Abbots Road. After a further 100 yards bear left at the battle waymark down Abbots Walk between houses. This takes you alongside a large cemetery and out into a park area to the south of Tewkesbury Abbey, known as Vineyards. You have now entered the Lancastrian lines which extended across the A38 back towards Bloody Meadow. On the left is a stone commemorating the battle and the Abbey. Stay on the tarmac path now to the right of playing fields, go through a gate and turn left along a roadway then cross a bridge over a stream before turning immediately left through a car park to the Abbey. **❷**

Leave the Abbey by the main entrance path and you come out close to the City centre. If you wish, and you have the time, there is much to explore in Tewkesbury amongst its ancient buildings and streets. If you like boats there is a path up to the Marina on the north side of the City. Otherwise (or afterwards) cross over the road from the Abbey into Mill Street, at the end of which is Abbey Mill, constructed originally on this site in 1190 and rebuilt in 1793. There is an information board about it and the Mill Avon sluice adjoining. Do not cross the bridge – unless you intend to walk up to the Marina – but turn left in front of it through a park bordering the Mill Avon. The way continues between hedgerows to exit at a car park alongside the A38. Go through the car park to join the footpath along the main road for just a few yards before turning off right down Lower Lode Lane where you pick up the battle waymark again. **❸**

146

The lane takes you past the entrance to Bloody Meadow and the sewage works then you bear left at a waymark opposite the end of the picnic site. This is the point I suggested you make a note of on the outward route. The path runs to the left of a tree belt along the edge of the golf course and, where you reach a waymark by the entrance to a private house, keep left and follow the obvious route as the way dips down to the rear of the house and continues along the edge of the tree belt. You arrive at a point where the path swings left around the back of the second tee following the line of trees and, after 100 yards, diverts right in front of a 'private' sign over a stile to continue down the other side of the same line of trees. Do not take the Severn Way path through a gate but stay to the left of the tree line, now moving away from the golf course.

Keep ahead at a stile in a crossing boundary then cross another in the next boundary. When you reach the end of the field continue round the bottom edge passing a pond on your right. Ignore a stile on the right at the end of the pond but, at a waymark on a fence post a few yards further on, turn right over a hybrid between a fence stile and an ordinary stile then turn right again along the edge of the adjoining field. You pass the earlier stile we did not cross and walk along the other side of the pond before crossing a footbridge on the right to continue ahead in another field to the left of a hedge.

After about 120 yards cross another footbridge on your right where there is a choice of routes. Take the option ahead across an embankment to another stile in a crossing boundary with farm buildings off to the left. Cross the stile which takes you over a brook into a field where you stay more or less on the same line before looping left to cross another stile adjacent to a farm barn. Go over the farm driveway and another stile into the next field and bear left around to the rear of the barn and through a gate into the churchyard of Deerhurst Church. If you can, visit the church. It is also a Saxon foundation and a priory church rich in history with numerous architectural and ecclesiastical artefacts, including what is probably the finest Saxon font in existence. It is in fact a study in itself and a guide book and information sheets are available inside. Leave by the front entrance passing the attractive fourteenth century farm attached to the church, which was probably once a dormitory for the monks of the priory. On reaching the lane turn right and around to the starting point.

Tewkesbury Abbey

As you will already have appreciated, Tewkesbury Abbey is a magnificent structure. Internally, it is even more impressive, possessing a tranquil beauty and calm presence far removed from the harsh realities of modern life. It was not always so of course – the Abbey has had its fair share of upheaval in its 900 year history, including the aftermath of the battle when the Lancastrians sought sanctuary only to be dragged out by the victorious Yorkists and executed.

Like so many of its sister foundations, it suffered under the dissolution policy of Henry VIII but, mercifully, most of it was saved by the local people who successfully petitioned the king to sell it to them for use as their parish church. There is a wealth of history here and architectural beauty almost beyond compare. I will not even attempt to describe any of it but leave you to immerse yourself in this extraordinary place.

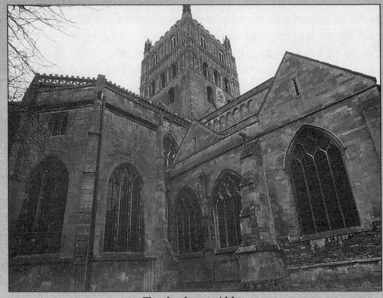

Tewkesbury Abbey

ENGLISH HERITAGE

No one does **more** for England's heritage

Join English Heritage and get three months' membership free

Magnificent castles ... historic houses ... enchanting gardens ... English Heritage membership offers you all the richness of our unique past, with so many glorious places to visit. Join today by Direct Debit* and you can receive three months' free membership. This means you'll be entitled to fifteen months' membership for the price of twelve.

Become a member of English Heritage and as well as making a personal contribution to protecting your heritage you'll enjoy:

- Free entry to more than 400 English Heritage attractions.
- Free or reduced price entry to around 500 special events.
- Half price admission to a further 100 historic properties in Scotland, Wales and the Isle of Man.
- A 248 page colour handbook with details of all our properties.
- A full-colour quarterly magazine, Heritage Today, to keep you up to date with projects we are working on.
- The opportunity to take part in special weekend breaks and cruises.
- A choice of exciting behind-the-scenes days.
- Priority booking and discounts on tickets for our summer season of outdoor concerts.

This offer applies to all types of annual membership:

Membership type	Annual fee
Adult	£31.00
Two adults	£50.00
Family	£55.00
Single parent family	£30.00
Senior citizen	£20.00
Two senior citizens	£33.00
Adult and senior citizen	£42.00

Prices valid until 31st March 2002.

To join English Heritage and receive three months' membership free, contact our Customer Services Department on: 0870 3331181 quoting reference DD6923/CH6924.

Other methods of payment are available. However, only Direct Debit payment qualifies for this offer.

Index

Index

Also by Roger Seedhouse...

Walks to Wet your Whistle

The walks in this book cover some of the most beautiful countryside in Shropshire and along its Staffordshire borders. From quiet rural backwaters to scenic hill country there is plenty to suit every taste. The book will appeal both to more experienced walkers and, by the introduction of shorter alternatives, to casual walkers or those wishing to vary the length of their walk as mood or time constraints dictate.

The eighteen main walks of between 7 and 11½ miles are arranged with a pub break conveniently located as near to half-way as possible. Short alternatives start and finish at the pub and range in distance between 2¾ and 5¼ miles.

The pubs vary in style and character but have generally been chosen to provide a watering hole in which the walker will feel comfortable, rather than for plush surroundings.

ISBN 1 869922 41 7. 112 pages. £6.95. 17 photographs. 18 maps.

More Walks to Wet your Whistle

Following the highly successful *Walks to Wet your Whistle* Roger Seedhouse here presents a second collection of eighteen walks covering some more of the most beautiful countryside in Shropshire and along its border with Staffordshire.

As in the first book there is plenty to suit every taste with main walks of between 6 and 10½ miles having a pub break at about the half-way stage and shorter alternatives of between 2½ and 5 miles starting and finishing at the pub.

ISBN 1 869922 36 0. £6.95. 112 pages. 24 photographs. 18 maps.

Available from booksellers or directly from the publishers (please add, for postage and packing, £1.00 per book).

Meridian Books

40 Hadzor Road ● Oldbury ● West Midlands ● B68 9LA